"Allen White's small group coaching opportunity was such a blessing for our congregation and my own spiritual, professional growth. Our staff was able to further streamline ministries and identify areas where greater potential existed."

—**Tiffany Danley, Christ Lutheran Church, Overland Park, Kansas**

"The *Exponential Groups* material is a masterfully done, complete small group primer that is easily used in any small group setting. I have been coached by Allen and have used this material to better myself and the groups ministry I lead. I would recommend the book and workbook to anyone serious about growing their discipleship ministry."

—**Steve Stringham, Cornerstone Church, Athens, Georgia**

"I've been a pastor in the Miami area for nearly forty years, and in that time, I have had the great honor to be trained by Allen White in coaching exponential groups. Allen is extremely professional and strategic in his approach to coaching, and my time with him was instrumental in the growth of our groups as well as our recruiting of new group leaders."

—**Rudy Rivero, New Dawn Church, Miami, Florida**

"If you are looking to expand your knowledge about small groups and breathe new life into your small group ministry this is the workbook you have been waiting for! Not only will Allen give you the tools you need to be successful in your ministry, but he will also walk you through the process step by step. Thank you, Allen, for changing our small group approach and for your expertise."

—**Jerry McQuay, Christian Life Center, Tinley Park, Illinois**

"Allen's coaching group provided us with hands-on learning from his vast experience. We were given practical tools, such as how to encourage people to get connected in groups and how to make us a church that builds groups—not just a church that offers studies."

—**Mike Willis, HighPoint Church, Lake Wales, Florida**

"It has been a privilege to be a member of Allen White's coaching group for small group ministry. His wisdom and insight on all things small groups has been a great blessing to our ministry. I am confident you will find great coaching and encouragement from Allen in this resource."

—**Jimmy Herndon, Second Baytown, Baytown, Texas**

"Allen White stands at the forefront of small group ministry. His coaching brings you to the cutting edge of small group ministry and helps you connect countless people to authentic Christian community."

—**Michael Hayes, St. John's Lutheran Church, Orange, California**

"Wouldn't it be great to have *all* the people in our churches connected to groups in which they can do life together, learn about God, and encourage each other? The problem is that we might be standing in the way of that happening without even knowing it. If you want to learn how to empower your people to step up and serve, and effectively reach those outside of the church, pick up a copy of *Exponential Groups* by Allen White. Your people have the power to impact the lives of others for God in the long term, and you can help them discover it."

—**Greg Surratt, Founding Pastor, Seacoast Church**
President, Association of Related Churches, author of *Ir-Rev-Rend*

"Allen White eats, sleeps, and breathes small groups and the strategies that help churches engage and connect their people. His experience is rich, broad, and deep. Not only will his stories of success inspire you, but his stories of what hasn't worked will also give you confidence in his advice. If you are serious about groups, this book will give you plenty to chew on and encouragement for the journey."

—**Rick Rusaw, Lead Pastor, LifeBridge Christian Church, Longmont, Colorado**
Author, *The Neighboring Church* and *The Externally Focused Church*

"What you'll find in the pages of this book is time-tested strategy to exponentially multiply your small group ministry. Allen has the heart of a pastor, the wit of a stand-up comedian, and the experience of a professional football coach. If you are a senior pastor or a small group champion and want to take your ministry to the next level, I would order this book for yourself and your entire leadership team."
—**Brett Eastman, Founder and President, Lifetogether Ministries**
Author of the *Doing Life Together* curriculum series

"Allen has written a terrific book from the seat of a practitioner. Having helped countless churches start and maintain small groups ministries, Allen's voice is one to be trusted. But beware: Read this book only if you're ready for your small groups to grow!"
—**Steve Gladen, Saddleback Church, Small Groups Pastor**
Author, *Small Groups with Purpose* and *LEADING Small Groups with Purpose*

"All of us learn from others. Allen has had the opportunity not just to learn from the best, but to be with and work alongside the best. No other small group book that I have read in my lifetime has captured the principles and practices of generations of group gurus as has *Exponential Groups*."
—**Rick Howerton, Church Consultant for the Kentucky Baptist Convention**
Author, *A Different Kind of Tribe: Embracing the New Small Group Dynamic*

"Pastors know that Christ-centered groups make thriving disciples. The hard part is developing a clear, workable strategy that empowers leaders, launches groups, and connects people. Allen's book just made the hard part a whole lot simpler! A true gift."
—**Bill Donahue, best-selling small groups author and leadership coach**

"I'm thankful Allen White has leveraged two decades of leading, launching, coaching, studying, and unleashing the power of small groups. Every church leader who would like to take their small groups ministry to the next level will benefit from his insights and experience."
—**Gene Appel, Senior Pastor, Eastside Christian Church, Anaheim, California**

"If you're ready to take your small group ministry to the next level, Allen White's *Exponential Groups* is a perfect playbook. Very few people have Allen's deep experience in helping small group ministries grow exponentially."
—**Mark Howell, Pastor of Communities, Canyon Ridge Christian Church**

"I don't know anyone who has worked with more churches on maximizing their small groups than Allen White. In *Exponential Groups: Unleashing Your Church's Potential*, Allen takes that wealth of experience and breaks it down for every church to easily digest and implement immediately. If your goal is to connect a lot of people into community in a short amount of time, then this book is for you."
—**Chris Surratt, Discipleship and Small Group Specialist**
LifeWay Christian Resources
Author, *Small Groups for the Rest of Us*

"*Exponential Groups* is a powerful, biblical resource that puts Allen White's decades of experience leading group life into your hand. No matter the size of your congregation, Allen's mindset and hard-won strategies will open a new chapter in the life and growth of small groups in your church community."
—**Herbert Cooper, Senior Pastor, People's Church**
Author, *But God Changes Everything*

"*Exponential Groups* brings to light a plethora of ideas and practices for the small group point person. You will walk away with new approaches to your small group system as Allen shares transparently from his ministry's successes and failures. Allen communicates the foundational structure of small group ministry in three sections. Strategy, Launch, and Structure have the added guidance of statements such as 'This is not your work,' which is a bolstering statement that clarifies for readers the need to share the load of small group ministry."
—**Eddie Mosley, Small Group Pastor, LifePoint Church, Smyrna, Tennessee**
Author, *Connecting in Communities: Understanding the Dynamics of Small Groups*

WORKBOOK

EXPONENTIAL GROUPS
UNLEASHING YOUR CHURCH'S POTENTIAL

WORKBOOK

EXPONENTIAL GROUPS
UNLEASHING YOUR CHURCH'S POTENTIAL

ALLEN WHITE

FOREWORD BY
CHIP INGRAM

an imprint of Hendrickson Publishing Group

Exponential Groups Workbook: Unleashing Your Church's Potential

© 2020 Allen White

Published by Hendrickson Publishers
an imprint of Hendrickson Publishing Group
Hendrickson Publishers, LLC
P. O. Box 3473
Peabody, Massachusetts 01961-3473
www.hendricksonpublishinggroup.com

ISBN 978-1-68307-269-0

All rights reserved. No part of this book may be reproduced or transmitted in any form or by any means, electronic or mechanical, including photocopying, recording, or by any information storage and retrieval system, without permission in writing from the publisher.

Scripture quotations contained herein are taken from the Holy Bible, New International Version®, NIV®. Copyright © 1973, 1978, 1984, 2011 by Biblica, Inc.™ Used by permission of Zondervan. All rights reserved worldwide. www.zondervan.com The "NIV" and "New International Version" are trademarks registered in the United States Patent and Trademark Office by Biblica, Inc.™

Printed in the United States of America

First Printing — April 2020

Contents

Foreword by Chip Ingram — ix
How to Use This Workbook — xi
Introduction — 1

The Strategy

1. Launching — 5
2. Aligning — 14
3. Weighing Risk — 22

The Launch

4. Coaching — 35
5. Recruiting Leaders — 52
6. Initial Training — 66
7. Connection Strategy — 78

The Structure

8. Sustaining Groups — 91
9. Leadership Track — 97
10. Coaching and Training — 103
11. Tracking Growth — 116
12. Beyond Alignment Series — 125

Appendix

Sample Sermons for Promoting Groups and Recruiting Leaders:

"Community in Christ" by Pastor Don Wink
Lutheran Church of the Atonement, Barrington, Illinois — 135

"The Connection Commandment" by Dr. Tony Evans
Oak Cliff Bible Fellowship, Dallas, Texas — 139

Notes — 147
About the Author — 148

Foreword

Small groups are a big part of what we do at Venture Church in Los Gatos, California, and at Living on the Edge, where we've witnessed hundreds of thousands of people start groups all over the world. Over the years I've seen a lot of small group strategies and big ideas come and go. I've seen some pastors practically wreck their churches to start small groups. I have also seen big group launches start with a bang and end with a whimper. But small groups are far more than a church program or ministry methodology. As I wrote in my book *True Spirituality*,

> Small groups are a means; authentic community is the goal. Authentic community is powerful. Authentic community is something we all long for. Authentic community goes way beyond simply being on a team or being a part of a club. Authentic community occurs when the real you shows up and meets real needs for the right reason in the right way. It's when the love of Christ is shared and exchanged with vulnerability, sacrifice, and devotion. It's a place where you can be just who you are and be loved in spite of your struggles, hang-ups, and idiosyncrasies.

And small groups are the container in which authentic community is formed.

None of us wants to create something new for the sake of something new. We want effective strategies that will grow our people and expand the kingdom of God, a place where people experience life on life and have the freedom to grow their gifts. Our people don't need more hoops to jump through. They need a place where they can connect in community in such a way that their faith grows, a place where grace is extended to others and real disciples are made.

A little while back, I met Allen White. He has served churches and groups for over twenty-five years, both as a small group pastor and as a coach to well over one thousand churches across North America. One of those churches was mine. We started four hundred new small groups in a single church-wide campaign, and then saw many of those groups continue on.

In this book, you will find a balance between new strategies and respect for what is already working in your church. You will see how you can build something new alongside something old and live to tell about it. Above all else, you will see how your people can become an army of leaders to create authentic community in your church to impact your city or town.

Allen offers practical insights and proven steps to start new groups in your church, whether you've been at groups for a long time or are just getting started. These are principles from the trenches, not unproven theories. What Allen has done in his own churches and in our church will work for your church as well. This isn't a cookie-cutter strategy that treats every church exactly the same. No two churches are really the same. The variety and flexibility you will discover in this book will help you make a custom fit for your congregation.

The end result isn't bragging rights about statistics related to how many people were connected into groups. No, the end result is far more important than that. Your people will experience community, mature in their faith, and become difference-makers in their world, for the glory of God.

Chip Ingram, Senior Pastor, Venture Christian Church, and Teaching Pastor, Living on the Edge

How to Use This Workbook

The purpose of this workbook is to put together all of the concepts from *Exponential Groups: Unleashing Your Church's Potential* (Hendrickson, 2017). This is a systematic approach to small group ministry. Using only part of the system will give a church only a partial result. Using the entire system for recruiting leaders, forming groups, establishing a coaching structure, offering a next-step study, developing a leadership pathway, and tracking metrics that matter will help a church start and sustain a large number of new groups. While the model is customizable, it works most effectively when all of the elements mentioned here are implemented by a church.

This is a workbook, which means it's time to get to work! While there is some new or updated information added since the printing of the original book, the value of this workbook lies in the exercises, timelines, templates, and examples given throughout. The purpose is not to give more information but to implement.

Since this workbook is intended to be used as a companion to the original book, *Exponential Groups*, the chapters of the workbook correspond with the chapters of the original. In this workbook, additional information from *Exponential Groups* will be noted as (*EG* [page number]).

> *I am aware that different churches will use different terms, so here are a couple of definitions for this workbook:*
>
> **Alignment Series or An Alignment** — This is a small group curriculum that aligns with a sermon series for the purpose of recruiting new leaders and connecting people into groups. In this workbook, an Alignment Series signifies a church-wide campaign, 40 Days series, or small group launch.
>
> **Small Group Pastor** — I use this term to signify the church's point person for small groups, whether this is a small group director or pastor, staff, or volunteer position.

Introduction

Exponential growth comes in two different ways. The common view relates to a trajectory. For example, eight people in a group each launch their own groups after a season. Eight times eight is sixty-four. This is the second generation. Then, when sixty-four people launch their group of eight, there are five hundred and twelve. The word *exponential* is generally applied when an organization reaches the third generation and beyond. Although I appreciate this thinking, there is a problem as not every culture is amenable to regular group multiplication. Small group pastors use terms such as "multiply" or "birth," but for many people it feels more like "splitting up" or "getting a divorce." Obviously, these are not good associations for most people. Some intentional disciple-making groups succeed at multiplying groups to a point, but in North America this is rare across an entire congregation. Most people are simply not willing to give up their group in order to start another.

So, if groups aren't exponentially multiplying, then why is this book title *Exponential Groups*?

There is another way to view exponential growth. Groups become exponential when you add an exponent to your goal. If you set out to start ten groups (or a hundred) in the coming year, the challenge is to multiply your goal by ten. Those reaching for ten groups would strive for one hundred groups instead. And if you're going for a hundred groups, then you stretch your goal to a thousand groups.

Does this sound farfetched? Ask Troy Jones, pastor of New Life Church in Renten, Washington, who started five hundred groups in a church of twenty-five hundred. Ask Jerry Branch, pastor of Dallas Baptist Church in Dallas, Pennsylvania, who connected a hundred people into groups in a church of fifty people.

If you think it's impossible, then it's impossible for you. No one has ever accomplished anything they perceived as impossible. When our church, New Life Christian Center in Turlock, California, went from having about two hundred and forty of our eight hundred people in groups to connecting over a thousand people in groups, it seemed impossible to others. Truthfully, when only 30 percent of our adults were connected into groups, I thought it was impossible too. We were stuck. So how did we connect 125 percent of our average adult attendance into groups? It required a change in our thinking.

I used to think that in order to have a hundred groups, I needed a thousand people. After all, a hundred groups multiplied by ten people each is a thousand people. But I was looking at this the wrong way. In order to have a hundred groups in a church, you need only a hundred people to start a group. If you have a leader, then you have a group.

Kingdom Life Church in Baltimore, Maryland, launched a video-based series called *Back to Church* in their church, which had a weekend attendance of six hundred adults. Before the series started, they had seven groups. When the series started, they launched a hundred and sixty-seven groups. These weren't ultra-small, small groups. Out of six hundred regular church members, one hundred sixty-seven stepped up to start a group. It's not impossible. It's exponential.

Your choice is to grow your groups exponentially or incrementally. While incremental growth seems easier, I can say that there was a year I didn't launch any groups, and I know I'm not alone. For any church to start five to ten new groups is pretty easy. But what if you multiply that number by ten? What if you embrace the possibility of starting fifty to one hundred groups instead? Rather than just connecting your congregation, you could connect your community.

An exponential group launch begins by challenging your incremental goals. Here's a little exercise for you to try before you start this workbook. Take a piece of paper and write down how many groups you plan to start in the next twelve months. Then take that number and multiply it by ten! That is an exponential goal. It's certainly more than you can accomplish on your own. It's a goal you cannot accomplish apart from God's intervention. This goal should scare you a little bit. This goal should overwhelm you. This goal should force you to take groups outside the four walls of your church into neighborhoods, workplaces, soccer fields, and commuter trains.

Launching exponential groups is far more than goal setting and strategy implementation. Working with proven strategies in this book, you will gain the tools to create the right environment for exponential groups, but the "exponential" part of this doesn't come from just following steps. You must have faith to achieve God-sized goals. Pray that God will give you and your church faith to recruit the leaders you need. Pray that God will help you raise the value of groups and motivate your people to connect. Pray that God will give you the coaches and the team you need to support your groups. Strategy without prayer is powerless. Doing the work of God without the power of God is a frivolous enterprise. Pray about every piece and every move.

Allen White
Simpsonville, South Carolina
April 2020

The Strategy

Chapter 1

Launching

Now that you have your goal in mind, it's time to roll up your sleeves and get specific about where you're headed in the next year as a church. In this chapter, you will create a definition of a group in your church and then look at the current involvement of your members and attendees in groups.

Should the church focus on connecting the people in their congregation into groups first or connecting people in the community into groups? The answer is yes! You can do both. In fact, you will connect people in the community into groups long before some of your slower moving members will join a group.

What Is a Group at Your Church?

Let's get practical and assess the current groups and classes in your church, and determine what your church needs and what your church can offer to your community in the next year.

What is a group at your church? *(Hint: Not every meeting or team is necessarily a group, and that's okay.)* Take some time as a team to define what a group is in your church.

1. How many people should be in a group? Determine a minimum and maximum number. Think about the ability for every member to contribute to a conversation. How big is too big? How small is too small?

Minimum Number: _____   Maximum Number: _____

2. How often does a group need to meet to qualify as a group in your church? *(Hint: Frequency is one factor in deepening relationships. The more often the group meets, the better the relationships. I do not recommend for a group to meet less than twice per month.)*

Your group will meet (circle one):
Once per month   Twice per month   Weekly   (fill in the blank) _____

3. How long is a typical group meeting? Most effective groups meet for ninety minutes to two hours to allow plenty of time for discussion as well as social time for the group members to connect.

How long should your group meetings be? (circle one)
1 hour   1.5 hours   2 hours   (fill in the blank) _____

> **4.** What should be included in your group meetings? (circle all that apply)
>
> | | | |
> |---|---|---|
> | Bible content | Discussion questions | Prayer |
> | Personal sharing | Testimonies | Refreshments |
> | Social time | Worship | Inviting others |
>
> What else? _____
>
> **5.** What should your groups do throughout the year? (circle all that apply)
>
> | | | |
> |---|---|---|
> | Service projects | Vacations | Missions trip |
> | Start new groups | Block parties | Day trips |
> | Sporting events | Concerts | |
>
> What else? _____

How long should a group last? The typical group life cycle lasts for eighteen months to two years. Some churches ask their groups to renew their commitment at the eighteen to twenty-four-month mark, while others encourage groups to disband at this point. Some groups, however, can last for decades.

The issue comes down to the amount of truth-telling in the group. Initially, groups are highly honest with one another, but over time they can become too comfortable. As the members get to know one another, they may become more lenient, especially toward sinful behavior or attitudes. If this happens, then the effectiveness of the group devolves. If the group can continue to challenge one another and hold everyone accountable, then the group can go on.

Another factor in the longevity of a group is whether they continue to invite and include new members. Every group will atrophy over time. If the group does not invite new members, then the group size will dwindle to just a few people. As time passes and the group has more history together, it becomes more difficult for them to add new members. Once a group falls below the minimum size you've determined for your groups, it needs to disband. These members should not join together to start a new group, because the dynamic will prohibit its growth.

Groups that continue to invite and include new members can last almost indefinitely. I started a men's group called Allen's Out to Lunch Group, which I led for four years. At the end of that time, only one original member remained, yet the group maintained about ten men. I passed the leadership over to one of the group members, Jeff, who led the group for the next four years. New members joined the group. Some older members stayed, while others moved on. Then Jeff passed the leadership on to a member of the group I don't even know. That group still continues, but I'm pretty sure they've changed their name!

> **6.** How long should your groups last? (circle all that apply)
>
> | | | |
> |---|---|---|
> | One study | One semester | 18–24 months |
> | Renew at 18–24 months | Indefinitely | Truth-telling |
> | As long as groups are growing | | |
>
> Something else? _____

7. Where should groups meet? (circle all that apply)

    On campus   Off campus   Homes
    Workplace   Coffee shops   Bookstores

    Somewhere else?_____

8. When should groups meet? (circle all that apply)

    Any day and time   During worship services   During midweek activities
    Monday   Tuesday   Wednesday
    Thursday   Friday   Saturday   Sunday
    Morning   Afternoon   Evening   Other: _____
    As the leader and group determines

9. What other expectations do you have for your leaders and groups? (circle all that apply)

    Report attendance   Check in with a coach   Report prayer requests
    Report group member issues Create a group agreement Share ownership
    Identify potential leaders

Create Your Group Definition

Now it's time to put your answers together into your group definition. Add your answers from the previous questions to create your definition.

At _____, a group consists of _____ to
         (church name)   (minimum size)

_____ people. Groups will meet a minimum of _____ times per month for
(maximum)   (answer from Q2)

_____ hours. During the meeting times, groups will _____
(answer from Q3)

_____. (answers from Q4)

Additionally, groups are encouraged to participate in the following over the course of a year:
_____. (answers from Q5)

Groups are expected to last _____. (answer from Q6)

Groups will meet at _____ (answer from Q7)

on _____. (answer from Q8)

Group leaders are expected to_____
_____. (answers from Q9)

What Groups Do You Have?

Now that you have created a definition for what constitutes a group in your church, list all of the groups, classes, teams, and activities in your church on the following chart. You should include Sunday school classes, electives, serving teams, Bible studies, men's prayer breakfasts, women's gatherings, singles' activities, membership classes, your assimilation pathway or growth track, D-groups (discipleship groups), free market groups (hobbies and interest groups), support groups, sports and recreation groups, online groups or Bible studies, classes such as Financial Peace University, leadership training, and so forth.

Please note: This exercise is intended to define groups, not to eliminate classes, teams, or activities that are currently working for a segment of your congregation. While you may embrace an emphasis to form groups and deemphasize other classes or events, you don't have to stop or curtail anything currently meeting a need. In fact, you should reassure these other classes, so they don't feel threatened by the emphasis on groups. Everyone does not need to be in the same system. After all, there is no one system that works for everyone.

This exercise should clearly point out that not everything in your church qualifies as a group according to your definition. That's okay. Some types of groups may have a different format, such as support groups. Other types of classes or teams should be challenged to take on more of the character of a group. For instance, if you have a Sunday school class that offers teaching with the class members seated in rows, you might want to change the room. Have the class members sit at round tables and shorten the teaching time to allow the table groups to discuss a few questions during the class. If you have hobby groups that focus solely on an activity, you should challenge them to add a devotional, testimony, or prayer time. If people are already gathered in classes, teams, or activities, is there a way they can become more like a group that fits your definition?

Please note: The last thing you want to do is cause these non-groups to feel threatened in any way. They may not be onboard with such groups. That's okay. Let what's working for them continue to work for them. The last thing you want is for these non-groups to be against groups. That's trouble you just don't need!

▲ **Your Groups** ▼

Group	Size	Frequency	Meeting Length	Meeting Activities	Longevity	Location	Is this a group?	Reason

Setting God-Sized Goals Exercise

What's the difference between a goal and a God-sized goal? It's simple. Your goals require a lot of focus and hard work. God-sized goals require big faith. We'll start by considering your weekly attendance and then imagine what it would be like to connect everyone into groups. If you really want to go for it, then substitute your attendance from last Easter instead as Easter attendance is probably a more accurate picture of who calls your church their church.

Follow the steps below to set your God-sized goals. Since many people may attend more than one group or classes, don't worry about duplicates on your list at this point. Once your group number matches your worship number, then you can focus on that.

Average adult worship attendance: _____
(If students or children attend your worship attendance *and* have groups, then include them in this number. If they do not have groups, then do your best to include only adults in this number.)

Current group members (based on your definition above): _____

Adults in other on-going groups or classes: _____

People who need groups: _____
(Subtract group members and members of other on-going groups or classes from your average adult worship attendance.)

New group leaders needed: _____
(Divide the number of people needing groups by eight.)

New coaches needed: _____
(Divide the number of new group leaders by three.)

Now, the question is whether you will accept this mission.

▶ *Case Study* ◀
Ward Church

Ward Church is a sixty-three-year-old Evangelical Presbyterian Church in Northville, Michigan, which is a suburb of Detroit. Ward currently has a congregation of eighteen hundred adults and has a long history of small groups.

The church offers a wide variety of groups to their congregation and neighborhood—groups for men, women, couples, singles, and parents. They also have a number of support groups, including GriefShare, Celebrate Recovery, and DivorceCare. Yet even with all of these groups, Ward had not connected their entire congregation into groups. They then chose to use an alignment series.

"People really enjoyed the series," reported Janet Branham, the director of their small groups. "An alignment series solved the question of what groups are going to study. It provided an opportunity to start new groups and get new people plugged into both our new and established groups."

With a long history of groups, the church needed a little finesse to get established groups onboard with the alignment series. "We have lots of groups that want to do their own thing and follow their own schedule," Branham shared. "Some complained that the material wasn't 'deep' enough. We added a digging deeper section to the curriculum to serve these groups and avoid this objection. We encouraged our existing groups to do the material and asked them if they had room for new people. If they chose to do the alignment study, then their groups were included in the church's Small Group Fair. We also made an appeal for new leaders to launch groups at the Small Group Fair."

By inviting rather than mandating, Ward Church was able to enlist many of their established groups. By honoring the established groups and even blessing those who chose not to do the study, Ward has been able to maintain a solid percentage of groups, both on campus and off campus, for decades.

Exponential Groups Timeline

Week of	Group Strategy	In Service Promotion	E-mail	Other
Launch -8			Send video to core members	Create host briefing packet
Launch -7	Identify influencers to "coach" new hosts			
Launch -6	Sneak peek meeting for existing group "coach" recruitment		Send to established leaders from senior pastor	
Launch -5	Create response card/ text message system	Series promotion video	Send to core church members from senior pastor	
Launch -4	New leader recruiting: briefings/orientations	Show promo video 1	Send promo 1 video midweek	Group sign-up form; create group signs/list
Launch -3	New leader recruiting: briefings/orientations	Show promo video 2	Send promo 2 video midweek	
Launch -2	New leader recruiting: briefings/orientations	Show promo video 3	Send promo 3 video midweek	
Launch -1	Small group connection event (optional) Group open house (optional)	Announce in worship service to connect in groups		
LAUNCH!	**Series launches week 1 Small Group Connection**	**Small group table for late members**		
Week 2	Group meetings	Small group table	Create host mid-series survey	
Week 3	Group meetings (mid-series host survey/huddle)	Promote next series		
Week 4	Group meetings			
Week 5	Group meetings		Create feedback survey; create "coach" survey	
Week 6	Group meetings			
Post-Series	Curriculum feedback survey; "coach" survey			

Launch Timeline Instructions

(See the *Exponential Groups* book for the full details and strategies that match this timeline)

1. Let's start at the "Launch" date. There are three ideal times of the year to launch groups: fall (August-October launch), the New Year (January-February launch), and Easter (groups are launched on Easter Sunday or the next Sunday). (See the "When to Align" section in *EG* 38–40.)

2. From the timeline, let's work backward. Just prior to the group launch, it's important to offer an opportunity for people who haven't been invited to join a group to meet the group leaders and sign up for a group. This replaces passive methods such as sign-up cards, websites, and small group directories. (For more details, see "The Most Effective Methods of Forming Groups" and the following sections in *EG* 128–35. For an understanding of this methodology, read all of chapter 7 in the book.)

3. Prior to forming groups, of course, you will need group leaders. So starting at least one month out from the group launch date, you need to begin recruiting group leaders/hosts/friends (whatever you want to call them) to lead groups. I recommend asking the senior pastor to make the invitation from the pulpit during the service, have the ushers collect the response in the service, and then you provide a briefing for new leaders after the service. You will also want to present some sort of video to promote the curriculum, recruit leaders, and promote the groups in general. Testimonies work best. (See *EG* chs. 5 and 6.)

4. Prior to recruiting leaders (denoted as the week of "Launch -7" in the example), you will need to prepare the videos to promote groups as mentioned in #3 above and some way for potential group leaders to respond in the service: sign-up card, text service, or mobile survey, etc.

5. Before you think of recruiting leaders or forming groups, you need to begin your coaching structure. The future of your groups depends on the support of the group leaders. You will find coaches from your current group leaders, elders, and other mature believers. Invite them to walk alongside the new leaders from the briefing (see #3) through the end of the series and then evaluate their experience. (See *EG* ch. 4 for more on this.)

6. Let's skip down to the beginning of the launch. I have found that on the day of the group launch and even the second week of the series, you will have people who haven't managed to get into a group. By providing a table in the church lobby, you can either introduce the prospective group members to a group leader who is still accepting new members or, even better, you can encourage the prospective member to gather a few friends and lead a group themselves. (See *EG* ch. 7.)

7. In "Week 3" from the example, you need to invite the new groups in the current series to continue into the next series. Don't give them choices. New groups won't have much of an opinion. The goal is to have the groups decide on continuing before the current study ends. You should be able to keep 80 percent of your new groups this way. Even if your next series isn't for a while, this will work. By sending a survey to the new leaders in the middle of the current series, you can get a feel for who will definitely continue, who won't, and who is undecided. Alert your coaches especially to those who are undecided. (See *EG* ch. 8.)

8. After the series concludes, survey all of the group members and get their feedback about the series. The survey could be as simple as: What worked? What didn't work? What's next? Also survey the experienced leaders who helped coach the new leaders. If they were effective and enjoyed coaching, then invite them to continue in this role. If they didn't like it or didn't do it, thank them for fulfilling their commitment. The trial run is now over.

Chapter 2

Aligning

The main purpose of an alignment series or a church-wide campaign is to identify and recruit new group leaders. While the church will connect many people into groups, this is a secondary purpose of an alignment.

Timing is a huge factor in an alignment series. Every church and community has key seasons of the year to recruit new leaders and start new groups. Every church and community also has obstacles to effective launches. By taking the rhythms of the calendar into account, most churches can effectively recruit leaders and launch new groups while avoiding obstacles.

For many churches, the "ministry year" in a large part models the public school year of August to May. Of course, there is some variation depending on school districts. The general rule is that when school starts, most people are back in church from summer vacation, Christmas break, or spring break. When school is out, then people are out. By observing the rhythms of the calendar, small groups can thrive. A typical American Launch Calendar looks something like this:

Seasons	Fall Series	Christmas (Group Life)	New Year Series	Spring Break	Easter Series	Summer (Group Life)
Dates:	Sept–Oct	Nov–Jan	Feb–March	March	April–May	June–Aug
Your Dates:						

The church's fall launch must be preceded by at least four weeks to recruit coaches (chapter 4), recruit group leaders (chapter 5), and form groups (chapter 7). (See the Timeline on page 12 to plan a specific launch schedule.) With this in mind, recruiting new leaders should start when most people are back in church after summer. This varies by community.

One year, I coached churches that launched their "fall" series at various times. The earliest was a church in Kentucky that launched their series on the second weekend of August. The latest was a church in New Hampshire that launched the second weekend of October. That particular year, I had a church launching a series every weekend in between except for Labor Day weekend.

The right launch date depends on your church. In some churches, groups must be offered when school goes back into session. Otherwise, family calendars quickly fill with school activities and there is no room for a group. In other communities, church members want to squeeze every bit of good weather out of summer before cold weather hits. In these cases, the launch should start later in the calendar. If people aren't regularly attending until after Labor Day, then start recruiting new leaders after the holiday and launch in October. This works as long as the series ends by Thanksgiving in the United States. Canadian churches should consider launching groups after their Thanksgiving and wrap up the series by late November.

Another important consideration is when the church will launch its follow-up series after the alignment series. The follow-up series is not a big push like an alignment series, but it is significant in getting new groups to continue (*EG* 165–71). If the fall alignment series starts in August or September, it is possible to offer a follow-up series in October to November. If the fall alignment series is later (October to November), then the follow-up series cannot start until January (or the New Year series is possibly the follow-up series).

▶ *Case Study* ◀

Vertical Church

Vertical Church is located in West Haven, Connecticut, and began over thirty years ago. The worship attendance is sixteen hundred adults in a diverse congregation made up of thirty-eight different nationalities. No one ethnicity is dominant. Prior to implementing the principles found in *Exponential Groups*, the church had thirty-four groups following the Free Market model of groups.[1]

"The verbiage in the Northeast is small groups don't work here," says Randal Alquist, the church's discipleship pastor. "Nobody wants to open up their houses. You're not going to get them to join. We're not a front porch community. We're a back deck community with fences. We're going into our backyards and have our own little space."

After digesting the content of *Exponential Groups*, the church was challenged to add a new approach. "My biggest revelation was this idea that people are already in groups," Alquist said. "There are distinctives we want to accomplish within a group. We want people praying together, people gathering together for community and to draw closer to Jesus. We're activating faith together in the group. If we know that's happening, and they're attending church regularly and serving once in a while, then we know they're growing. This revolutionized my approach in how to talk about groups and promote them."

Previously, the church sought out people with high qualifications to lead a group. The new leaders were given a fifty-two-page manual they were expected to follow. Alquist says, "We started giving people permission to jump in. We're asking for people who love people and love God. We're not asking for elders here. We want people who are willing to facilitate a healthy environment where connections can happen." The fifty-two-page manual was eventually replaced with a ten-page manual and a short briefing meeting at the church, and training videos were created to answer common questions from the small group leaders. Each new leader received a coach to help them.

In their most recent alignment series, Vertical Church had over ninety groups with nine hundred twenty group members. Additionally, another two hundred forty people are involved in eight short-term Growth Groups at the church. "This approach opened up a world to us," Alquist enthused. "We knew community was happening on the periphery, but we've been able to look at all of these little communities in our church and identify some basic things for those leaders to start practicing and to make sure it's happening. It's been amazing."

Possible Obstacles to an Alignment Series

Sometimes in scheduling a series of alignments, your church will face obstacles to a series that runs six consecutive weeks. There are certain things on the church's calendar or even community events that will conflict with the alignment series. While this isn't cause for alarm, you should at least be aware.

These types of "obstacles" include missions conferences, service weeks, revivals, conferences, and other events. Write the types of events and their dates in the space below.

Event	Date

Troubleshoot the Obstacles and Consider Possible Work Arounds

1. Can the event be moved or postponed?

2. If the event involves the weekend services, can the alignment series be delayed for one week to accommodate the event and then resume after the event is over?

3. Can the small group study continue even if the weekend service does not align with the alignment series topic that week?

Worst Case Scenarios

If there are several competing events during the six-week alignment series, the rhythm of the series will be thrown off. If this is the case, then the church could choose to delay the series until another time. The alternative is to use the weekend services to launch the series, and then the small groups do the study apart from the sermon topics used on the weekend.

If the church is hosting a conference, then launch small groups based on the topic of the conference. For instance, if the church offers a parenting conference, start groups on parenting. The same is true for marriage conferences, men's or women's conferences, or other topics. Use the event to start groups. Not only will the church gain groups, but conference participants who truly desire to make changes will have a better chance with the continued focus, support, and accountability of a small group.

If events frustrate the church's efforts for an alignment series, sometimes the answer is in embracing the frustration. Whether the church launches groups with an alignment or launches groups from the "obstacle," the net result is additional new groups.

Group Life during Nonalignment Seasons

Small groups are not just about group meetings. In fact, group life might be more significant than some group meetings for a couple of reasons. First, group members getting together outside of the group meeting indicates that they like each other. This is the kind of community the church wants to see, and these are the types of relationships where iron can sharpen iron. What happens outside of the group will largely determine what happens in the group meeting. But groups need to know they can and should connect outside of the meetings.

Groups don't necessarily need permission to gather outside of their regular meeting times, but they might need direction. As a rule of thumb during nonalignment seasons, such as the Christmas season (which in the United States is from Thanksgiving through New Year's Day) and summer, the church can offer options for groups to gather at least once per month to offer opportunities for continued group life. Groups can meet socially, serve together, or host an open house. (For more ideas, see *EG* 165–71.)

The second reason groups should do things outside of meetings is that not all spiritual growth takes place in association with a study. While Bible studies give direction for life, times outside of group meetings offer an opportunity to try on the principles learned in the group meetings. After all, the goal of the group is to create well-rounded disciples whose actions and attitudes reflect what Scripture teaches. It's one thing to learn about the Good Samaritan. It's another thing to be a Good Samaritan. Even unguarded social times can allow for a deeper understanding of each other. The more the group members know each other, the more freedom they will feel to open up in the group meetings.

At least one month prior to scheduled breaks in meetings, such as Christmas or summer, church staff should offer suggestions for how the group can gather outside of their regular group meetings. Many groups will do this naturally, but some might need a reminder or a nudge in the direction of meeting socially during the break.

Not every group will take a break from meeting. I led a men's group that met every Wednesday for lunch fifty-two weeks of the year. Although there were times when attendance was low, we always got together. This was a good pattern for our group.

Some churches will offer a summer session for groups that extends into midsummer. If this is a church's regular pattern, then it should continue. In some cases, however, a summer session could create a diminishing return for the church's fall group launch. Often a summer break will create more momentum for a fall launch. The church should decide the best approach for their members for a summer session. If the church discovers a loss in momentum for the fall alignment, then an adjustment should be made.

> **Nonalignment Season Exercise**
>
> 1. What is your church's normal pattern for group meetings?
>
> 2. How well is the current pattern helping group members accomplish the group's goals?
>
> 3. If group goals are not being accomplished, how might you adjust the schedule?
>
> 4. Considering the current alignment schedule or group semesters, when should the church communicate options for nonalignment seasons or semester breaks?
>
> 5. What types of activities can be suggested to groups for these breaks?

Choosing the Right Topic for an Alignment Series

If people are not already attracted to your community or haven't figured out how to get connected, then the right topic can be the first step toward experiencing biblical community. Think back to when you made friends in school. Sometimes that happened because you had a lot of classes together with the same people. The right topic can have a similar effect in helping people find community in the church. (For more on this, read *EG* 30–31.) Here are a few things to consider in choosing a topic.

Who Is the Church Trying to Reach?

- *Everybody:* Think about a broad topic such as purpose, significance, stress, spiritual growth, relationships, or something similar. Two examples of good books to use include *One Month to Live* by Chris and Kerry Shook[2] or *Holy Ambition* by Chip Ingram.[3]
- *Couples:* Married or considering marriage.
- *Parents:* New parents, parenting stages, or stepparents.
- *People in life transitions:* Newly married, new parents, separated or divorced, widowed, relocation, new careers, laid off, newly retired.
- *People struggling with life-controlling problems:* Those dealing with addiction, bad habits, etc., who need support.
- *Who else?*

In most cases, a church cannot reach everyone with the same campaign. That's okay. The idea is to identify more potential leaders and connect prospective group members. As discussed earlier in this workbook, successful alignments are done in a sequence. Each group launch will build on the next until everyone in the church is connected.

What Is the Senior Pastor Passionate About?

Over the years, I've counseled small group pastors and directors who were wearing themselves out trying to get their senior pastor onboard with groups. I would tell them, "It's your senior pastor's boat. You need to get onboard with him!" God speaks to the senior pastor and directs the church. If the senior pastor is heading in a direction that might not make the best topic for an alignment series, that's okay. The best alignment series are always the ones the senior pastor is the most passionate about. What is your pastor passionate about? How can you align groups with where your pastor is headed?

What Are Major Themes in Your Pastor's Ministry?

While pastors hopefully preach the whole counsel of God, most pastors have favorite themes they are the most passionate about. In fact, you can probably think of the names of well-known pastors who are known for teaching on purpose, leadership, relationships, evangelism, or other topics. What are the common themes in your pastor's ministry?

Pastors have no shortage of content. They have years or even decades of sermon files. When you think of topics for an alignment series or even creating your church's own curriculum, these major themes in your pastor's ministry can point you in the right direction.

A pastor in Bakersfield, California, wanted to create a book, study guide, and video teaching for a series on relationships. His assistant and small group pastor pulled sermon files from the pastor's office. They returned with an enormous box full of sermons on relationships, marriage, parenting, and other related topics. These files were then organized into an outline for the book, study guide, and teaching videos.

Pastors don't need to create the next *Purpose-Driven Life* best-seller.[4] They can draw from their passions and make a big impact on their church, community, and beyond. A box of sermons isn't even necessary. In fact, I've helped pastors create small group curriculum from one sermon series or, in some cases, a couple of sermons. After all, for most curricula, only six to eight minutes of video teaching is needed, and then the study guide is written based on the videos.

What are your pastor's dominant themes? Do a quick review of the video archives on the church's website. Ask other staff or church members what they would say are the pastor's main themes. Talk to your pastor directly about it. Then gather the materials and get to work on repurposing the content for the series.

Creating Your Own Curriculum

There are some distinct advantages to a church creating its own curriculum (which are outlined in *EG* 34–37, 42–45). The largest advantages are that self-produced curricula increase the interest of both your senior pastor and your church members in the series. That's a win/win in most cases.

Producing and writing curricula requires a significant amount of work. Over the years, I have either produced, directed, or written series for Rick Warren, Chip Ingram, Doug Fields, Tony Evans, Sheryl Brady, and dozens of other pastors and churches. While most of these projects were created with either a production crew I hired or church staff that I coached, I have also worked with church members who volunteered their time and skills to create curricula.

There Are Several Options When It Comes to Creating Curriculum for a Church

1. Of course, you can always use production services from Allen White Consulting (we would be more than happy to help!) or a similar curriculum production company. There are a handful production companies that specialize in creating small group curricula. They can offer scripting, production services, curricula writing, and graphic design. There is usually an option either to have the production crew travel to you or to send your pastor to them. Most curricula can be turned around in thirty to forty days and will be print-ready. The disadvantage is the cost.

2. Some churches have their own staff audio/video teams. The advantage is that the church already has a trained video crew and the equipment necessary for creating the video teaching. There can be struggle sometimes with the video team's availability. While shooting a series in the summer for a fall launch is easy, shooting in the fall for a New Year's series can be more challenging. While this option is more affordable, there will be a learning curve to creating curricula. Coaching is available to teach churches how to produce their own curriculum. Another issue that often comes into play is that the person overseeing the project, typically the small group pastor, has no authority over the production team. In this case, departments must cooperate to produce the series. But sometimes this is easier said than done!

3. Some churches hire a local videographer who shoots advertising, weddings, or other events. While the church will need to prepare the content on their own, a local videographer can take all of the responsibility for the shoot, the crew, the equipment, and the post-production. The cost will vary. The only disadvantage is that the videographer will not initially understand the genre of small group curriculum. But, with the church's direction, a quality product can be developed.

4. Many churches have either professional or amateur videographers, graphic designers, writers, or project managers within their own congregation. By asking for volunteers or surveying the congregation, churches can identify who has interest or ability in these areas.

Once prospects are identified, they should be assessed to determine their specific abilities and the quality of their work. Most pastors know that just because someone likes to sing, it doesn't mean they should join the worship team. Most videographers post streaming videos online. Many writers have a blog. Ask these prospects to supply a sample of their work to see if what they do will mesh with what the church needs.

Once people are secured for these roles, ask them to participate in one project. Don't give permanent roles to contributors until you experience what it's like to work with them and what they can produce. If they do a great job, then invite them to help with other projects. If they were difficult to work with, missed deadlines, or produced poor work, then thank them for their commitment and move on.

The advantage of working with church members is that the cost will be low, even with some equipment rentals. The disadvantage is that since people are volunteering their time, the projects tend to take longer, especially the first one. In this case, you will need to allow plenty of time to complete the project and hold each person accountable to their deadlines.

Sample Video Production Timeline

Here is a sample video production and writing schedule with distribution occurring during the New Leader Briefings. In this particular scenario, curriculum production begins eighteen weeks prior to the series launch. Some parts of the timeline will vary in length, and the amount of video content will affect the amount of time needed for video editing. The final output of the curriculum also has some bearing on the schedule. If a church is producing printed study guides and DVDs/steaming video, then time must be allowed for printing and duplication as well as delivery if the printer and DVD duplicators are not located in your town. If the church produces only downloadable resources, of course, then no time for printing, duplication, or delivery is needed.

Week of	Video Production	Print Production
Launch -18	Pre-production meeting	Select printer and book format
Launch -17	Recruit on-camera roles: leader training, testimonies, session host	
Launch -16	Create video scripts	
Launch -15	Secure shoot location and necessary equipment	
Launch -14	Any additional planning and preparation (optional)	
Launch -13	Video shoot of six teaching segments, six session hosts, four to six testimonies, and six leader lifters. Shoot video promotion (in service or via e-mail) for (1) recruiting and (2) series promotion	*Writing:* Attend video shoot and take notes; begin creating lesson questions from shoot info and scripts *Graphics:* Design page template; assemble intro pages and appendix
Launch -12	Video editing	*Graphics:* Design branded covers and DVD menu *Writing:* Edit your writing template for relevance
Launch -11	Video editing	Writing
Launch -10	Video editing	Writing
Launch -9	Video editing, DVD authoring, edit promo videos	Graphic design and layout
Launch -8	Review DVD proof/final DVD masters	Proof layout and create print-ready master
Launch -7	Duplication	Printing
Launch -6	Duplication	Printing
Launch -5	Delivery	Delivery
Launch -4	Distribution begins/new leader briefings	Distribution begins/ new leader briefings

Chapter 3

Weighing Risk

One of the primary purposes of an alignment series is recruiting potential group leaders. The other primary purpose plays into the first one: engaging the senior pastor. As we've discussed, when the sermon series is linked to the small group study or, even better, when the pastor's teaching is the basis of the curriculum, the pastor will be more interested in groups. When pastors make the investment in creating small group curricula, they want to make sure it is used to its full potential and they want as many people to lead groups as possible.

While there are other good reasons for an alignment series, such as the whole church studying a topic together and getting more people into groups, all of this rests on the number of leaders a church will recruit. The more limitations the church puts on who can lead a group, the fewer leaders the church will recruit. Fortunately, the reverse is also true, but who is the church getting?

Attempting to recruit a large number of leaders is a two-edged sword. On one side is the desire to provide a quality group experience with a qualified group leader. The other side is the simple fact that most people don't consider themselves to be any kind of leader. As soon as you bring up the word *leader*, many people will decline your offer. They want to help but not necessarily lead. Many churches have found it helpful, therefore, to do away with the term "leader."

In the early days of church-wide campaigns such as *40 Days of Purpose*, Saddleback Church chose to call people H.O.S.T.s instead of leaders (see *EG* 12–14). This took away the sense that people were being asked to do more than they felt qualified to do. The churches I served used this strategy, and it worked for a while. But after using the term "Host" in campaign after campaign, people became wise to the idea that "Host" really meant "Leader." The jig was up. Now what?

Many of the churches I've worked with have dispensed with the terms "leader" and "host" altogether. While many have struggled with what to call these folks, others have recruited for the function of a group leader without using the term. The invitation would sound more like, "Get together with your friends and do the study." While the pastor was actually inviting people to "lead" a "group," neither of those terms were used, and yet people would gather a group of friends and do a study together. This just means that everyone is already in a group after all!

This is more than a ruse to get admitted non-leaders to lead groups. In fact, churches should be stingy with the term "leader." In the Bible, commissioning someone as a leader was a significant proclamation. As we see when Paul writes to Timothy, he says, "Do not be hasty in the laying on of hands" (1 Tim. 5:22). The sense here is that before someone is commissioned as a leader, they must prove themselves. It's not enough just to select the "right" people and thoroughly train them; the church also needs to see them in action. Do they have the stuff to lead? In most cases, the church won't know until they've actually seen the potential leader in action—actually leading something. Thus the dilemma: if the church has a high standard for leadership, which they should, and the people they are attempting to recruit do not consider themselves to be any kind of leader, then how do you recruit a significant number of leaders? The answer is that you don't.

Let's take this beyond semantics. This is not a debate of what to call someone or even of lowering the bar on leadership to the point where small groups seem unimportant because so little is expected. The dilemma speaks to the importance of a recruitment process that will bring in the maximum number of potential leaders possible, without putting the church leadership into a scenario that bears an uncomfortable level of risk.

> ▶ **Case Study** ◀
>
> ## New Dawn Church
>
> New Dawn Church is a bilingual congregation of two hundred adults in Miami, Florida. Senior pastor Rudy Rivero leads worship services in both English and Spanish, and the church offers English, Spanish, and bilingual groups, which they call Circles.
>
> Despite a long history of groups at the church, there were still people who were not connected into groups. It was therefore time to try something new. "I had not used video-based curriculum in any of the groups before," admitted Pastor Rudy. "It was really the highlight, because for those six weeks, we started six new Circles. We discovered that the Spanish groups loved the journey with the videos. They're asking for more. It was easier to engage in terms that the facilitator doesn't have to feel the pressure and can just ask the questions."
>
> The church took two approaches to recruiting more group leaders. First, they approached the existing Circles and asked if anyone would be interested in leaving their Circle to start a new group. Four people took them up on this offer. Then the pastor challenged the entire congregation to start their own Circles. Two couples, who had never participated in groups before, stepped up to start a group for the first time. Out of the six new groups the church started, half of those continued after the series. The members of the groups who chose not to continue joined other groups. Overall, more people participated in groups during the alignment series than ever before and are continuing on.
>
> In addition to increasing the overall number of groups and members, the church also gained one new permanent coach, bringing the total to three coaches, as well as having a handful of temporary coaches who could be called upon for future church-wide studies. "We have formed a little hub of people we can go back to when we open other circles," Rivero added. "Now I can use these seasoned people on a more permanent basis as coaches."
>
> Using video-based curricula and inviting the congregation to start Circles, however, was not good news to everybody. "Our leaders gave a little bit of pushback," Rivero confessed. "The thought of opening a Circle from the perspective of someone who was new or possibly unsafe was a scary thing for my people. But, once they understood it, this was really good."
>
> For this smaller, bilingual congregation, this was a risk. But their risk paid off. "My only obstacle," said Pastor Rudy, "is I want to go faster than what we're doing, but I guess going slow is a good thing because it does create more of a solid foundation."

Levels of Leadership

Many churches have resolved this issue by adding a separate category for group leaders who have not fulfilled all of the requirements for leadership in their churches. Some have designated their leaders as "Level 1 Leaders," who are new recruits leading a group for an alignment series, and "Level 2 Leaders," who have met the qualifications the church established for small group leaders. Another church offered the labels of "Series Group Leaders" for the new alignment series leaders and "Small Group Leaders" for leaders of on-going groups who met the church's leadership requirements.

Levels of leadership offer the potential for admitted non-leaders to have a trial run leading a group without the designation of "leader," since they must prove themselves before they can be called "leaders." The alignment series is an opportunity to offer this trial run for people to have the experience of leading a group short term so they can decide whether or not they enjoy leading a group, and the church can evaluate their ability to lead. The big question now is what your church will require of those who agree to a trial run.

Let me make one more distinction in these categories of leadership. Some churches have found a certain safety in not advertising groups whose leaders the church leadership does not know well or who are unproven. Often, groups that respond to an invitation to "get together with your friends and do the study" are not publicized in any way. They don't appear in a group directory or website, and they are not represented at a connection event or small group fair. It's up to the leader to recruit 100 percent of the group members out of their friends, family, coworkers, neighbors, acquaintances, and others. The assumption is that the people being invited know the person who is inviting them and have an idea of what they might be getting themselves into. Rather than referring to these as "Closed Groups," I prefer to call them "Invitation-Only Groups."

When a church advertises a group or the group is represented at a connection event or small group fair, there is an expectation that the church is endorsing the "leader" of a group. As stated previously, there are some issues with offering this designation too early—the most basic of which is that the church cannot endorse someone they do not know.

For our purposes here, I have defined the three categories of small group leadership in the exercise below as:

- *On-Going Group Leaders:* Leaders who have been commissioned and designated as leaders officially by the church.

- *Advertised "Hosts":* Groups that are open to receive sign-ups and participate in connection events that are led by "unproven leaders," who have yet to meet the qualifications of the first category of leaders.

- *Invitation-Only Groups:* Groups led by unproven leaders that are not advertised. These groups are formed by personal invitation only and are not publicized by the church in any way.

Exercise: Your Church's Current Small Group Leadership Requirements

In the chart below, typical requirements for small group leaders are listed in the left column. This list is not meant to prescribe what type of requirements your church should have for your leaders. It is simply a compilation of common requirements used by churches in general. There are some blank spaces for you to add any additional leadership requirements specific to your church.

Review the list of requirements, and then put an X in the next column, "For On-Going Leaders," to indicate all of the requirements the officially recognized group leaders in your church must meet. Read the next section before you designate the requirements for the remaining leader classifications.

Requirement	For On-Going Leaders	For Advertised "Hosts"	For Invitation-Only Groups
Breathing/willing			
Confession of faith			
Baptism			
Church membership			
New leader briefing			
An interview			
Coaching			
Basic leader training			
On-going leader training			
Potential leaders			

The Significance of a Trial Run

A trial run provides the church with some grace. It's not a permanent designation, which is helpful for both the church and the prospective leader. An admitted non-leader might consent to try a short-term assignment, such as leading a group for a six-week series. In the meantime, the church can evaluate the prospective leaders' level of interest and abilities. If they perform well, then the prospective leaders can be invited to do more. If they don't do well or don't enjoy leading a group, then there is a designated ending point to the short-term commitment.

If leading a group for the alignment series was not a good experience for the prospective leaders, more than likely they will not continue their groups. But for those who enjoyed leading their groups, unless they are given an opportunity to continue, their groups will also cease to meet.

The best way to get groups to continue is to offer a second study in the middle of the current study. If the follow-up study is not offered until the end of the study, then the group will usually disband, and it will be challenging to get them back together. By offering another study at the midpoint of the alignment series, the group has time to decide whether or not they want to continue. I typically advise churches to select a second study for the groups. The only decision the new group should face is whether they will continue. By selecting a study for them, it simplifies their decision. If there are exceptions, then consider those as exceptions.

What I am describing here is a larger recruiting process, and it starts with the trial run. I have discovered that most groups who successfully complete the alignment series and then continue into a second study will become on-going groups. They will enter into a small group life cycle (*EG* 197–99). Or, as stated in *Diffusion of Innovations* by Everett Rogers (*EG* 154–58), these leaders have completed the third and fourth stages of adopting a new idea and are ready for the final stage: confirmation. At this point, the prospective leaders have informally indicated by completing two back-to-back studies that they and their groups are open to staying together and continuing their journey. If the church has deferred any of the requirements previously, this is the time to reintroduce the requirements and invite the prospective leaders into a pathway to become officially recognized leaders by the church.

Stop Lowering the Bar on Leadership

In *Exponential Groups*, I made a lot of the idea of lowering the bar on leadership (chapter 5). The big idea is simply that most churches require more than is necessary to lead a small group and make disciples. In an effort to make the experience of group leadership easier for church members, pastors would often offer extensive training to prepare their leaders for any potential scenario that might occur in the course of leading a group.

Two problems surfaced with that approach. First, it's impossible to cover what to do in the case of every possible contingency. Second, too much information of what could happen in a group could actually worry prospective leaders and cause them to back out. The best approach is to allow group leaders to have the experiences for themselves and train them as they go. The pastors and coaches should be prepared to help the leaders, but the issue shouldn't be raised until the issue is present.

The requirements for a trial run are not nearly as extensive as the requirements for officially designated leaders, nor should they be. High requirements for a trial run become an obstacle to many prospective leaders, while low requirements become detrimental to on-going groups. There is cause to lessen the number of requirements initially without removing them completely. Lowering the bar is a good way to recruit prospective leaders, but there should be a point in time when these requirements are reintroduced.

Think of it this way. Have you ever bought a car? What's required to buy a car? To actually buy the car, there is a lot of paperwork. Your signature is required for the dealership's internal paperwork, for the vehicle's registration, and for the loan or lease of the vehicle. It's a great formula for writer's cramp.

The alignment series is not like buying a car. The short-term group experience is more like the test drive. What's required to test drive a car? I've purchased cars in three different states in my lifetime: Kansas, California, and South Carolina. In all three cases, the test drive required only two things: a valid driver's license and the salesperson riding along.

When it comes to prospects leading a short-term alignment series or some other trial run in your church, what is the "driver's license"? What are the minimal requirements? For churches I've served, as well as those I've coached, this has varied. In most cases, some of the requirements were delayed for the trial run and brought back later. In a few cases, all of the requirements were waved. For those churches that never brought back the requirements, there was a diminishing return (see chapter 12 of this workbook).

Go back to the chart on page 25 of this workbook and indicate what the "driver's license" is for the last two types of leaders: Advertised "Hosts" and Invitation-Only Groups. Knowing that eventually the church will bring back certain requirements for these types of leaders to become On-Going Leaders in your church (as signified by column 2), which requirements are deal breakers for the church and which requirements can be waved temporarily?

Requirements and Results

The number of requirements for prospective leaders is inversely proportional to the number of prospective leaders a church will recruit. Simply put: more requirements mean fewer prospective leaders, and fewer requirements mean more prospective leaders. You won't have high requirements and an overabundance of new prospective leaders. It just doesn't work that way.

Over the years, I've had conversations with several small group pastors who had the same thing in common: they were all former small group pastors at the same church, and they all left for the same reason. In theory, the senior pastor wanted everyone who attended the church in a small group. The problem was that there weren't enough groups for all of the church's members, and the requirements placed on new leaders created a stranglehold on the church's ability to recruit. Every leader had to be a member of the church, but there weren't enough members of the church interested in leading groups. Considering that the church had a high percentage of people who were not in groups and a relatively low percentage of people who qualified as leaders, the small group pastors faced an impossible situation and eventually a new career. The senior pastor needed either to lower his expectation for how many people should be connected into groups or lower the requirements for small group leadership (at least temporarily). After several conversations with this pastor's former small group pastors, my sense was that the pastor was really not serious about connecting his church into groups. (If this sounds like you, call me. I can help.)

Is It Possible to Lower the Bar Too Far?

I believe it is possible to lower the bar too far in two different ways. The first is when the church leadership, or even the small group pastor, is placed in a situation where they are highly uncomfortable. Maybe the requirements have been lowered to the point that it brings extreme anxiety to them. As I wrote in *Exponential Groups*: People typically don't find a lot of success in promoting something they fear. They can actually be relieved when they have a poor result. There is less to be afraid of (*EG* 52).

In one incidence, a senior pastor wanted to increase the number of groups in his church from about one hundred to four hundred in an alignment series. They created curriculum based on the pastor's teaching. They lowered the bar. They recruited for three weeks in a row. They reached their goal. But the small group pastor kept saying to me, "I can't wait until this gets back to normal." He's no longer on staff at that church. The next year, the church added a hundred more groups and had five hundred groups in their alignment series.

When a church lowers the bar, they have to be ready for the result. It's one thing to be a little apprehensive in taking a risk. It's another thing to be terrified of it. Pastors should not let anyone convince them to go way beyond where they are willing to go—not even me. Each church must choose its own acceptable level of risk.

The second way of lowering the bar too far is by not addressing prominent issues in the prospective leaders' lives. This is a more difficult line to define. On the one hand, the church doesn't want to put someone in a dangerous or inappropriate situation. On the other hand, the church also doesn't want to issue a laundry list of disallowed behaviors. While some things are a matter of sin, others are a matter of conscience. And even in the case of sin, who is without it?

I believe there are two areas that can prove detrimental to both prospective leaders and their potential groups: relationship issues and life-controlling problems. Even in these situations, I prefer to evaluate these circumstances on a case-by-case basis. There is, however, a place for standards to be implemented without becoming legalistic in the approach.

Overall, my concern has always been for the person who is struggling. This concern is over and above what they can do for the church. If someone is going through a marital separation or divorce, then I want to make sure he or she is receiving the help and counsel needed during a very difficult time. If a couple is cohabitating but is not married, then that would be cause for a conversation (see *EG* 49–52). If a person's lifestyle is not compatible with the values of your church, then a pastoral conversation about where that person is in their journey would be in order. If someone is struggling with a life-controlling problem—whether it be substance abuse, addiction, pornography, or something else—then a support group or counseling would take precedence over small group leadership.

Please understand that none of this should be taken in a punitive sense. As a pastor, you are putting personal needs ahead of the church's need for leaders. This is probably a time when they should join a group rather than lead one. Sometimes people will want to distract themselves by focusing on the needs of others to keep them from focusing on their own needs, but this is not a healthy form of leadership.

I used to dread these conversations, but then I discovered that I was given an opportunity to bring up a subject that either I was unaware of or didn't have the opportunity to talk about previously. I'll be honest: While not all of these conversations went well, they were necessary and many people found health, hope, and recovery.

How do you know what someone is dealing with? When our church opened the door wide to potential leaders at a church I had served for twelve years, I had a pretty good idea of what was going on with our people. For those I didn't know as well, I had a team of experienced leaders who helped me coach them.

When I arrived at a new church of over six thousand where I barely knew anyone, I e-mailed the entire list of prospective group leaders to the entire staff and asked if anyone had any hesitations about anyone on the list. The staff gave their feedback, but in reality, there weren't very many concerns.

Additionally, in the recruitment process, the prospective group members were asked to give some background information (see the "Leader Information Sheet" document in chapter 6 of this workbook on page 74). The final question addressed the concerns listed above: "Is there anything going on in your life that could potentially harm or embarrass the church or bring shame on the name of Jesus?" Then there were two specific categories:

1. Current habitual struggles or moral issues (an addiction, cohabitation, a sexual relationship outside of marriage, or similar).

2. Current marital struggles (infidelity, separation, divorce in process, or similar). Churches will vary on their definitions of what might fit into these categories.

The criteria for prospective leaders should be based on the church's values and interpretation of Scripture.

Who Qualifies?

I have discovered from the two churches I served and the hundreds of churches I've coached that the problems amount to about 2 percent. If I had a hundred new leaders, then I would need to talk to two of them. This has been consistent. And, again, it gave me the opportunity for a pastoral conversation I might not have had otherwise.

The other thing I discovered was that some people weren't ready to admit what was going on in their lives. We typically gave an information form at a briefing for the alignment series. Those who weren't prepared to discuss what was going on with them simply left the briefing without turning in their information sheet. They did not pursue leading a group either. Technically, there were more than 2 percent who struggled with that last question on the information form, but they didn't identify themselves. In a different way, the purpose was accomplished, but unfortunately those who didn't acknowledge their personal need could not receive the help they needed immediately.

Exercise: Who Qualifies?

Going back to the chart on page 25, review the requirements for each of the three types of leaders. Approximately how many people in your church would qualify for each category based on the requirements you have set forth? Write this number in the bottom row of the chart.

Are these numbers you can live with? If you would like to have additional potential leaders, then you will need to adjust the requirements to allow for more prospective leaders. Here is a rule of thumb for each category:

- **Breathing/Willing**: 98 percent since 2 percent will have issues we just described.
- **Confession of Faith, Baptism, and Church Membership**: The number depends on the church. For the 80 percent of churches that are plateaued or declining, this number is probably over 90 percent.[5] For churches that are dramatically growing and experiencing revival, this number would vary greatly.
- **New Leader Briefing**: If the church only distributes curriculum at the briefing, then the church will easily acquire all of their prospective leaders here.
- **An Interview**: This can become a bottleneck depending on who is allowed to conduct the interviews. If these conversations are with coaches, then more interviews can be conducted in a timely way.
- **Coaching**: Going back to the Setting God-Sized Goals Exercise on page 10 in chapter 1, the number of coaches is limited only to the number of available and willing experienced small group leaders and mature believers in the church. From this exercise, the best potential coaches are in column 1, "On-Going Leaders." We will discuss this further in the next chapter. It is my position that every potential leader should receive a coach. This is the "salesperson" in the test drive analogy.
- **Basic Leader Training**: This training focuses on what it means to be a small group leader at the church. This is usually offered in a one-time two- to three-hour format at the church. If prospective leaders are required to complete this before leading a group, then the requirement could cause a logistical bottleneck in terms of when the prospective leaders are available for training, when the training can be offered, and how many can attend the training at a time.

Here is an example of what a church that has two hundred members, but has five hundred people attending worship services, might look like for its first alignment. In this case, "On-Going Leaders" could include Sunday school teachers, Bible study leaders, and small group leaders.

Requirement	For On-Going Leaders	For Advertised "Hosts	Invitation-Only Groups
Breathing/willing	X	X	X
Confession of faith	X	X	
Baptism	X		
Church membership	X		
New leader briefing		X	X
An interview		X	
Coaching	X	X	X
Basic leader training	X		
On-going leader training	X		
On-going coaching	X		
Weekly reports	X	X	X
Number of potential leaders	15	25	490

What's Your Mindset?

One big thing stands between you and where you want your groups to go. It's you. When you consider the numbers in the last exercise, you probably fall into one of three categories of thinkers: it's impossible, it's interesting, or it's possible. If you think it's impossible, then it is.

When our church doubled our groups from 30 percent of the weekly worship attendance in groups to 60 percent connected into groups, then doubled again from 60 percent in groups to 125 percent in groups (all within six months), the biggest change was in my own thinking. My thoughts had to move from safety to risk taking. I had to stop making excuses for my perceived limitations and make room for those I considered to be unqualified to try leading. The exercise below will reveal how you think about reaching big goals and developing the small group ministry in your church.

Mindset Exercise

For each statement below, rank yourself as Strongly Agree, Agree, Uncertain, Disagree, or Strongly Disagree. The more honest you are, the more aware you will become of your mindset.

	Strongly Agree	Agree	Uncertain	Disagree	Strongly Disagree
1. I struggle to change and learn.					
2. I imagine a bigger future.					
3. There are some things I cannot do.					
4. I will become more in the future.					
5. I struggle imagining what's possible.					
6. Failing is a chance to learn more.					
7. I explain my life based on my past.					
8. I regularly try new things.					
9. I fear failure.					
10. I'm excited about my future.					

Scoring

If you indicated you Strongly Agreed or Agreed with the odd-numbered questions and Strongly Disagreed or Disagreed with the even-numbered questions, you most likely have a "fixed mindset."

If you indicated you Strongly Agreed or Agreed with the even-numbered questions and Strongly Disagreed or Disagreed with the odd-numbered questions, you most likely have a "growth mindset."

These concepts came from research conducted by Dr. Carol S. Dweck, as articulated in her book *Mindset: The New Psychology of Success*: "The view you adopt for yourself profoundly affects the way you lead your life. It can determine whether you become the person you want to be and whether you accomplish the things you value."[6]

People with a fixed mindset believe they must work with the hand they're dealt. "The fixed mindset creates an urgency to prove yourself over and over. If you have only a certain amount of intelligence, a certain personality, and a certain moral character—well, then you'd better prove that you have a healthy dose of them."[7]

People with a growth mindset, on the other hand, believe that what they currently possess is merely a starting point. They can grow. They can change. They can imagine a better future for themselves and others. "This growth mindset is based on the belief that your basic qualities are things you can cultivate through your efforts. Although people may differ in every which way—in their initial talents and aptitudes, interests, or temperaments—everyone can change and grow through application and experience."[8]

The good news is that regardless of which mindset you currently possess, you can change and grow if you choose to. If you're in more of a fixed mindset, then you will probably want to approach the thoughts in this book in small doses. Take small risks, and then take another one. You don't have to jump into the deep end to be successful, but you can't stay in the lounge chair either. If you're afraid of failure or blame, then hire me as your church consultant. If it doesn't work, then it's my fault!

I moved from a high control posture to a high growth position by gradually implementing different strategies to start groups, keeping what worked, and learning from what didn't work. Fortunately, more worked than didn't work and the failures weren't nearly as dramatic as the successes. I think the same will be true for you.

The Launch

Chapter 4

Coaching

In some circles, coaching is either underrated or nonexistent. I think this is a mistake. Coaching provides a number of helpful practices for new and established leaders:

- Support and encouragement
- Customized training targeted to specific needs
- A spiritual covering for ministry
- Supervision and accountability
- A resource to help meet the needs of group members
- A sounding board for new ideas and troubleshooting issues
- A relationship with a like-minded leader
- A link between the group and the church

While there are many more reasons why coaching is important, these are a good start. This chapter will offer the tools and strategies to start a coaching structure, and chapter 10 will explore developing a full coaching structure and offering relevant coaching to group leaders at various stages.

Where to Start

Start with new leaders. A completed organizational chart does not need to be in place to effectively coach leaders. In fact, I've seen some impressive charts that actually didn't represent very much. There wasn't a lot of coaching going on, but everyone was accounted for.

Since new group leaders need the most help, start with them. When prospective leaders show up at a briefing (see chapter 6), they can meet their coaches. The assumption is that every new group leader at your church gets a coach, and they should. New leaders are far more accepting of both the coaching and the help than established leaders. In fact, if you assign coaches to seasoned leaders, this will be met with everything from suspicion to resentment. Established group leaders will need a different style of coaching, which is covered in chapter 10.

New leaders will have many questions. As the church continues to implement new strategies of forming groups like the HOST model or "do the study with your friends," as mentioned in the previous chapter, two things will happen: (1) the "leaders" of these groups will be more and more less "experienced" and will need help, and (2) the church leadership will not be as familiar with these "leaders." As mentioned previously, the safety net here is launching non-groups led by non-leaders that are not advertised, but there is still a responsibility toward these non-leaders and their non-groups. If each of these prospective leaders, even in the unadvertised groups, has a coach, then the leaders will be supported in meaningful ways and the church will be assured of what's going on because the coach is checking in.

How to Recruit Coaches

In *Exponential Groups*, I write about my early attempts at recruiting coaches. Let's just say it didn't go so well. As I detail in the book, there were many issues—recruiting the wrong people, unclear expectations, a controlling small group pastor (me!)—stuff like that. Leaders would say yes to coaching other leaders, but they became bored because I was still coaching all of the leaders. Some of them said yes only because they couldn't tell me no. That, of course, didn't work, and I had to find new coaches to replace them. Then I faced a dilemma that changed how I recruited coaches.

Our church doubled its groups in one day, but I wasn't adequately coaching the groups I already had. Now I had twice the problem. Then it dawned on me that if we had double the groups, this meant that half of the leaders were new and didn't know what to do, while the other half had some experience, so I matched them up. I didn't even call them coaches. It was the "buddy system," and it worked well enough.

Since you're smarter than me, you're not going to wait until a crisis occurs to get all hands on deck. If an alignment series, church-wide campaign, or a semester can be trial runs for prospective group leaders to test drive a small group, then that short-term commitment could also be a trial run for experienced leaders to test drive coaching.

What to Expect of Coaches

I'm a fan of keeping the trial run simple. Below is a description of what to look for in prospective coaches and what to expect from them. Please note: I am reluctant to grant the title "coach" until the experienced leaders have proven themselves as coaches and completed the trial run. In the past, I've used terms like "partner," "guide," "experienced leader," and "buddy."

Small Group Guide Job Description

Qualifications

- Experience as a small group leader
- Interest and availability to walk alongside a couple of new leaders
- Availability to attend one to two New Leader Briefings to meet new leaders
- Report back to [supervisor: small group pastor or team member]
- Suggested: Recruit a co-leader for your group

Expectations

- Make a weekly call to the new group leaders starting with the briefing week until the end of the series
- Answer the new leaders' questions
- Encourage the new leaders
- Pray for the new leaders when you think of them

Preparation

- Honestly share from your own experience—good and bad
- Obtain a copy of *Leading Healthy Groups* by yours truly
- Optional: Follow the agendas provided

Sample Coaching Job Description

Here is a sample coach job description from Bay Hope Church in Lutz, Florida:

Bay Hope Coaching Quick-Start Guide[9]

Our expectation is that you will model for your group of leaders how you want them to engage with their group participants.

This means you, as a coach, will do the following:

- Continue to develop your personal relationship with God.
- Pray for your group.
- Communicate regularly with your group.
- Treat leaders with respect and concern.
- Promote confidentiality: Only report problems to the director of groups, not other leaders or coaches.

How many groups will I have and when do I communicate with them?

- Each coach will have one to two groups to work with.
- You will communicate with each group leader once per week. A phone call is the preferred method and will deliver the best results for both you and the group leader. A text message will work if necessary. An e-mail is the last resort.
- These conversations should take two to five minutes each.

When I am coaching a leader, what do we talk about?

- What was the best thing that happened in your group this week/best thing about your group?
- What is the worst thing happening in your group?
- Are there any issues with your group I can assist with?
- What study are you going to do next?
- How can I pray for you?

> **Examples of what to ask the group leader about their own spiritual growth:**
> - How is your personal relationship with God?
> - What are you doing to promote your own growth?
> - What devotional are you doing right now?
> - Do you use a Bible app? If so, which one?
> - What is the latest book you've read?

▶ Case Study ◀

Connect Church

Connect Church is an eighty-three-year-old Wesleyan Church of four hundred adults in Lawrence, Kansas. In recent years, they've started groups through church-wide campaigns for the first time and knew they would need help to support the group leaders with coaches.

"Before, we didn't have any kind of a coaching structure," said Elizabeth Scheib, connections and communication director. "I was caring for all of the leaders and not doing a very good job of it. I also tend to be a control freak. I wanted to control a lot of the processes and the things the leaders went through. But we were stuck. We had plateaued." The church at the time had an adult attendance of three hundred and fifty with a hundred sixty-five people connected in sixteen small groups. "It wasn't impossible to coach sixteen groups. It just wasn't effective, because the whole thing in coaching is about relationships."

As the church began to embrace the *Exponential Groups* strategy of creating their own curriculum and making the lead pastor the spokesperson for groups, they knew many people would respond to host a group. They also knew these new hosts would need help. "If the host came out of a group, then their former group leader naturally became their coach since there was already a connection." But many more people were about to host a group for the first time as well.

The established small group leaders were already in the practice of joining Elizabeth twice a year for a "huddle" (a phrase coined by Carl George in *Prepare Your Church for the Future*, meaning when group leaders meet for care, training, and accountability) prior to the two annual group launches. "I explained at the huddle that we wanted to grow our groups, so we were adding a layer to our structure called coaches. I asked them if they had a heart to come alongside a new host and help them get off to a great start; we needed their help. Then I explained the responsibilities and gave them a starter kit that included a coaching description and a coaching timeline" (see pages 39–44 of this workbook). Their leaders responded.

One new host almost immediately got cold feet after she had volunteered to start a group. "We asked those who wanted to host a group to come down to the front of the sanctuary after the worship service. We gave them the information about starting a group and matched them up with a coach."

In this case, a woman had talked herself out of hosting a group by the time she had left the sanctuary. "I can't do it," she said. "My husband is an introvert, and he never wanted to do it, but I felt like we should." Elizabeth encouraged the woman to give the group a chance. Her husband could be the "kitchen guy and hang back where the introverts hang out." She could lead the discussion. Elizabeth also encouraged her to talk to her coach.

When the coach called her, they talked for an hour. "It was laborious, but the coach was so gracious and had such a heart for this couple." They ended up leading a successful group for the eight-week commitment and even added a potluck each week so the husband had a valued role. "It would not have worked if they did not have constant encouragement and prayer from the coach."

Another couple decided to host a group. They were extremely gifted and had considerable experience leading groups. In fact, they were involved in campus ministries at local colleges. They still needed a coach to serve and support them—not in skills training but in their own journey as believers. "They knew how to lead a group. They were not foreign to this. But I also knew that if I was going to make the coaching structure work, I couldn't give them a pass. I couldn't be their coach. I knew from being in a women's group with the wife that they were going through some stuff." The couple was therefore matched with another couple who coached them. "I assigned them to coaches I knew would be able to really establish a deep spiritual relationship with them." Not long after the assignment, Elizabeth discovered the coaches had already called them, and they had gone to coffee together. While they didn't need someone to tell them how to lead a group discussion, they did need prayer, encouragement, and friendship. They didn't follow everything in the coaching timeline, but they received the coaching they needed.

By recruiting experienced leaders to coach new hosts, Elizabeth discovered the church could provide the care the leaders needed and she could provide the overall guidance for how the leaders were coached. By loosening the reins on coaching, the groups at Connect Church became unstuck. They went from plateaued to thriving.

Coaching Sample Starter Kit

Growth Group Coach[10]

Ministry Description

Growth Group Coaches want to see lives changed for Jesus in the context of relationships. A win for a Growth Group Coach is when their HOSTs[11]/Group Leaders and their group members take their next steps to worship Christ, grow as disciples, and serve their worlds.

Growth Group Coaches welcome and orient new HOSTs through the beginning eight-week HOST experience. They commit to an intentional "spiritual friendship" with HOSTs/Group Leaders in which they offer prayer, encouragement, and support in practical Growth Group situations.

Growth Group Coaches must be willing to commit to an intentional relationship with no more than five HOSTs/couples. They must be experienced Growth Group Leaders and support the mission of Connect Church Growth Groups to connect every person into a thriving group where they are cared for and urged to grow spiritually.

Approximate Time

The majority of time given to this role will focus on two growth group sessions: fall and spring. During a group launch, time given will average one to two hours per week. During "off" times of the year, time will most likely average less than an hour a week (prayer, monthly contact, etc.).

Core Responsibilities

1. Pray for and with HOSTs regularly.

2. Correspond with HOSTs as frequently as HOST process prescribes (or until HOST chooses to step out of the mentoring relationship).

3. Provide godly counsel to HOSTs.

4. Serve as a link between your Growth Group Director and HOSTs regarding issues that need support.

5. Attend the Coaches dinner for encouragement, support, and sharing.

6. Identify other potential Growth Group Coaches or HOSTs and share with them how you see God moving in them.

Are You In?

I commit to becoming a Growth Group Coach. I commit to mentor my HOSTs to live out Connect Church's Mission to worship Christ, grow as a disciple, and serve my world. I commit to faithfully carry out to all of the responsibilities required with this important position.

_____   _____
Name   Date

Connect Church also used the following document to script what prospective coaches should talk about with new leaders each week.

Sample Coaching Timeline

Connect Church, Lawrence, Kansas[12]

HOST Briefing/My HOST's Name: _____

Cell: _____   **E-mail:** _____

Day and time of group meeting
(so you can make sure and call them the day after): _____

Coaches Group on myCC (my Connect Church online database)

You are part of a group on myCC called "Coaches." There you can find files to download that may be helpful to send to your Hosts. There are also YouTube videos on Icebreakers, and myCCHow-To's where you can copy the links and e-mail them to your hosts. Just click on the Files tab. A copy of this timeline can also be found there.

Make Host Phone Calls

- As soon as they say "yes": Thanks for stepping up!
- Ask whether this is their first time hosting a group. This can help determine the level of care needed.
- Make sure they contact each person who signs up. This is critical.
- Ask if they are using myCC. This is the preferred method of group communication
- Get to know your host. You are a support resource, but more importantly you are there to develop a spiritual friendship. Ask about their family, profession, etc.
- Ask:
  o What questions do you have?
  o How can I pray for you?

First Meeting

- **Ready for first meeting?** (review first meeting info in Starter Kit)
- Send reminder e-mails.
- Inform everyone how they can get their discussion guides and reading plan (online or sanctuary exits).
- Potluck meal planned?
- Start thirty minutes early this week for the meal.
- Review the discussion guide and write down responses to each question.
- Don't have to be a Bible scholar; just stay one step ahead and grow along with the rest of your group.
- Look over your group agreement so you are familiar with it.

Have your meal, do an icebreaker, go over Group Agreement, pick questions from discussion guide (shorten the lesson this week)

- Be yourself! Pray for God to use you and your unique character and gifts.
- Share the load. You don't have to do everything yourself. (Dessert sign-up list, rotate homes, etc.)
- What questions do you have?
- How can I pray for you?

After First Meeting

Tell them to follow up with anyone who didn't show up. They need to assure their members it's not too late and that they were missed.

- What is going well?
- Struggles?
- Questions?
- How can I pray for you?

After Second Meeting

- What is going well?
- Struggles?
- Questions?
- How can I pray for you?

After Third Meeting

- How are you doing?
- What is God teaching you?
- How is God showing up in your group?
- How is group going? (discuss progress, problems, plans)
- How can I pray for you?

After Fourth Meeting (half-way through!)

- How do you feel?
- Are your group members beginning to gel? Are relationships developing?
- What is God teaching you?
- How can I pray for you?

COACHES DINNER MEETING [Insert date and time and location]: This will be a time to share how this experience is going so far, what you are learning, and fine tuning some of the things we are doing. Coaching is still new. The Connect Church staff wants to learn from you in this process.

Choose from the list of questions below based on the level of your HOST's experience. You know what they need or don't need, including how often to contact them. Maybe they only need a text message saying that you're praying for them; maybe they need a personal meeting. These steps are up to you. Whatever you choose, please contact them at the end of the session to thank them.

Week 5

- Review the journey: Have you enjoyed hosting your group?
- What did it feel like when you signed up to start a group?
- Who did God bring to your group?
- Any God stories to share?
- Will you consider hosting again for the fall session?
- If interested, let them know there will be Leadership Training.

Week 6

- Have you discussed what you plan to do as a "fun" night (the final night)?
- Throw out some ideas like a concert, movie, progressive dinner, and see what your group may want to do together.
- Even if you just start the last meeting thirty minutes early, include a meal to celebrate what God has done these last eight weeks.

Week 7

- Have you solidified your fun event or meal celebration? What are your plans?
- Talk to your group about continuing for the fall session.
- This session will begin in October.
- There is no pressure to continue—for you or your members. This was only an eight-week commitment. Discuss it as an option for those interested.

Optional: Invite your HOST out for a treat/coffee to thank them. Turn in receipts to Elizabeth and you will be reimbursed.

You can ask things like: What are some "God stories" from your group? Where did God show up for you as a host? Where did you see him move in the lives of your group members? Provide overall encouragement and gratitude.

Week 8

Hosting was a trial experience—a taste of group life. Do you think this role was a fit for you? Do you want to continue in the fall?

> **Next Steps**
>
> **If no:**
> - Thank them for investing in their group over the last eight weeks. Affirm what they have done to help build the kingdom and support our vision!
> - Ask if they have another person they would recommend to host the group
>
> **If yes:**
> - Invite them to step up to a Growth Group Leader.
> - Walk through ministry description with them.
> - Explain that they will be invited to Leadership Training in August.
> - This will not change anything they are doing with their group. The change from Host to Group Leader is in their personal commitment (given life to Christ, baptized, etc.), and training.
> - We want John 10:10 for them—full life!
>
> **With either response, affirm their eight-week commitment again.**
> - Thank them for investing in their group over the last eight weeks. Affirm what they have done to help build the kingdom and support our vision!
> - They are part of something bigger than just groups at Connect Church!
> - A small group of twelve disciples started over two thousand years ago, and God has been moving in people's lives ever since and will continue to do so.
> - Thanks for being part of God's story!

How to Recruit Coaches

Coaches can really be recruited at any time, but the most effective season is prior to an alignment series or group launch. Review the "Setting God-sized Goals" exercise in chapter 1 to determine the number of new coaches you will need to help the new leaders you plan to recruit.

It's easier to recruit prospective coaches for a trial run than for a permanent position. Most people are open to a short-term commitment. It's also better for you if the prospective coaches complete a trial run first. As you will see, some people have what it takes to coach. Others do not. At the end of the trial run, the effective coaches can be invited to do more coaching, while the ineffective ones can be thanked for fulfilling their commitment. You will have a better idea of how well an experienced group leader will perform as a coach when you have the opportunity to watch them perform. In the past, I've recruited people I thought would be stellar coaches only to discover they were either unable or unwilling to coach. Since I recruited them, I also had to release and replace them. A trial run is a fair test of someone's interest and ability to coach.

When it comes to coaching new leaders, any leader with any amount of experience is able to coach. They don't necessarily need to be years ahead, as long as they're a little ahead. A group leader in one church I served led a group for the first time in our fall alignment series and then offered to coach a new group leader in the New Year's series. How much experience does a group leader need to coach a new leader? At least six weeks!

Prospective coaches can be recruited in a couple of different ways. If the church is under a thousand adults, then look at your current leaders and ask yourself, "Which leaders do I wish I had ten more just like them?" Invite those leaders to walk alongside new leaders. You might also come across a few leaders you don't want to see duplicated (or you might not even want that group.) Don't invite them.

If the church has over a thousand adults, then you need a broader approach to recruit prospective coaches and a targeted approach to recruiting your small group team. The approach to recruiting the small group team is similar to the approach for recruiting coaches in a church of less than one thousand. You want to handpick well-performing group leaders and coaches to join the team.

The tone of the invitation has a lot to do with recruiting coaches. If the approach is a low key request such as "Would you be interested . . . ," then there will be a mediocre result. If a sense of urgency is added to the request, however, then the result will be much better. Here is how I have recruited dozens of new coaches:

> As you've heard, we are launching an alignment series this fall. As our pastor makes the invitation for people to host groups, we will be inundated with new leaders and our current coaching structure will be completely overwhelmed. I need your help. I need each of you to walk alongside one or two new leaders from the new leader briefing through the end of the six-week series. We're passing around a sign-up sheet with all of the dates and times for the briefings listed. Please plan to attend one or two briefings over the next few weeks to meet your new leaders in person and start helping them.

As the church prepares for an alignment series or group launch, gather the established group leaders together before you start recruiting new leaders. I call this meeting a "Sneak Peek." Essentially, this Sneak Peek is a briefing for established leaders. The purpose is to give these group leaders the first look at the new alignment series and to recruit them as prospective coaches. This both honors them for leading groups and takes the pressure off of the new leader briefings that will lead up to the series launch (see chapter 6 for more information on this briefing).

The agenda for the Sneak Peek can look like this slide deck from a previous Sneak Peek event I held for a series called *Living a Balanced Life*.

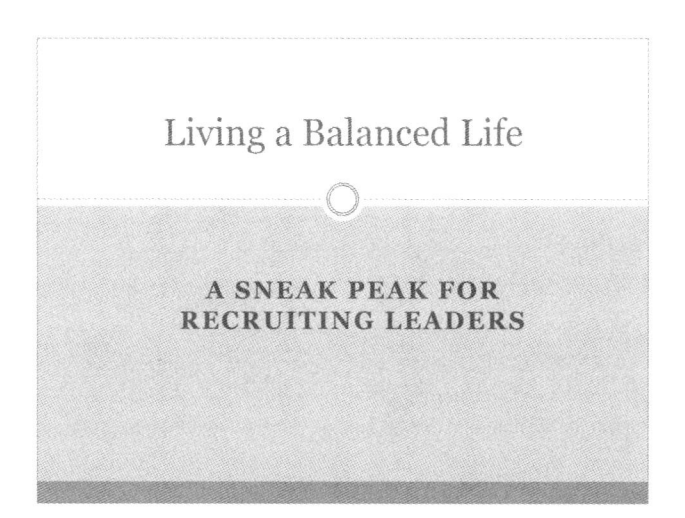

Living a Balanced Life	Series Details
A SNEAK PEAK FOR RECRUITING LEADERS	• SIX WEEKS: [INSERT DATES] • WEEKLY MESSAGES FROM OUR PASTOR • STUDY GUIDE BY ALLEN WHITE • WEEKLY VIDEO-BASED SMALL GROUP STUDY

When, Where, How . . .

- THE GROUPS WILL MEET WEEKLY FOR 1.5 TO 2 HOURS
- DAY: HOST WILL CHOOSE
- TIME: HOST WILL CHOOSE
- LOCATION: OFF-CAMPUS
- LENGTH OF COMMITMENT: SIX WEEKS
- REFRESHMENTS: WHATEVER YOUR GROUP CHOOSES!

Build Your Group

- INVITE YOUR FRIENDS
- USE THE SMALL GROUP POSTCARDS
- CONNECT AT SMALL GROUP CONNECTIONS: AFTER SERVICE ON SUNDAYS, [INSERT DATES]
- USE THE CHURCH WEBSITE

Get Online

- CREATE YOUR LOG-IN AT: [CHURCH WEB ADDRESS]
- E-MAIL: [CHURCH CONTACT]
- WITHIN 24 HOURS, YOUR PROFILE WILL BE CONFIRMED
- RECORD YOUR WEEKLY ATTENDANCE

Help a New Group Leader

- WALK ALONGSIDE ONE TO TWO NEW LEADERS DURING THE SERIES
- CALL THEM ONCE A WEEK
- ANSWER THEIR QUESTIONS
- REMEMBER TO PRAY FOR THEM

Sign Up

- MEET THE NEW LEADERS AT ONE TO TWO OF THE NINE NEW LEADER BRIEFINGS
- SIGN UP FOR THE DATES AND TIMES YOU ARE AVAILABLE
- START CALLING YOUR NEW LEADERS THAT WEEK

How do you get established leaders to attend the Sneak Peek event?

- Give each of your established leaders a free copy of the curriculum.
- Distribute the curriculum to established leaders at the Sneak Peek only.
- Offer free childcare.
- Provide a meal.
- Invite the senior pastor to cast vision for the series.

Sample Invitation to a Sneak Peek Event at a Church I Served

Dear Small Group Leaders and Previous Hosts,

Our pastor is planning a great new series this fall that includes a small group study. You are invited to preview the series at our Fall Sneak Peek on Wednesday, August 11, at 6:30 p.m. in Room C. Everyone who attends will hear our pastor's heart for this series and will receive a copy of the study guide and DVD or streaming access for their small group to review.

If you would like to attend, please register: [insert link]

Childcare is provided with a 48-hour advance reservation.

Don't miss out on this great new series!

God bless,

Allen White
Adult Discipleship Pastor

Sample "Love Letter" to Small Group Leaders: Coaching Invitation to Experienced Leaders

Dear Group Leader,

I want you to know that I love what you do. You are on the front lines of ministry. You are making disciples. You are fulfilling the Great Commission by opening up your home, gathering in a coffee shop, or leading a meeting at the church. Who you are is rubbing off on them! You are showing them how to imitate Christ in your own imperfect way.

This Valentine's Day, there is something I wish for you. I want you to have the help and support you need to carry out your ministry. Often you face questions or situations for which you don't have a good answer. You need someone in your corner. More often than not, you face discouragement or you may feel inadequate to serve the group God has called you to lead. And, on top of that, there is an enemy who wants to discourage and defeat you every step of the way. I don't want you to face all of that alone.

I am willing to help, but our church has more groups and leaders than one person can possibly keep up with. This Valentine's Day I wish for you a coach—someone with experience who is available to you, who will offer the help and support you need. Not only that, but there are leaders who could benefit from your experience whom you could coach. If you're not given a coach, then I invite you to ask an experience leader to mentor and help you—who would you invite?

Thank you for all that you do!

Love,

[Your Name]

Sample Prospective Coach Sign-Up Form
(create one of these to represent each of your new leader briefing days)

Supporting New Small Group Leaders	
Sunday [insert date]	**Sunday [insert date]**
After [insert time] Service	**After [insert time] Service**
After [insert time if there is a second service] Service	**After [insert time if there is a second service] Service**
After [insert time if there is a third service] Service	**After [insert time if there is a third service] Service**

How to Supervise Coaches

While at this point, the small group pastor's focus should be on enlisting prospective coaches to help with new leaders, it's important to bear in mind where this might be heading. An effective coaching structure will increase the support given to small group leaders and will decrease the amount of work placed on the small group pastor. This will take considerable effort to build, but once it's built, the dividends are tremendous and the model is exponentially scalable. The basis for the coaching structure is found in Jethro's advice to Moses in Exodus 18:13–26. (Read this passage before moving on.)

Just as we saw in this passage about Moses, it's also not good for all of the small group leaders to come to the small group pastor. In verses 15–16, Moses gave two excuses for his behavior, which are essentially: (1) the people like coming to me, and (2) I'm the only one who can do it. There is probably a larger lesson here on becoming codependent on ministry, but that must be saved for another book!

Based on Jethro's advice, Moses designates leaders of tens, fifties, hundreds, and thousands. In a small group coaching structure, the leaders of tens would be small group leaders; the leaders of fifties and hundreds would be coaches; and the leaders of thousands, if the church has thousands, would be a small group leadership team, which could be either staff or volunteer positions.

For a church with less than a thousand adults in groups, the coaching structure could look like this:

Small Group Pastor/Director
serves
Leaders of 50s & 100s = Small Group Coaches
serve
Leaders of 10s = Small Group Leaders

For a church with more than a thousand adults in groups, the coaching structure could look like this:

Small Group Pastor/Director
serves
Leaders of 1000s = Small Group Team or Staff
serve
Leaders of 50s & 100s = Small Group Coaches
serve
Leaders of 10s = Small Group Leaders

If you are just starting to recruit new leaders in your next alignment series or group launch, you do not need to have this entire structure built or every leader accounted for on the organizational chart. But keep this structure in mind as you are starting your coaching structure, because this is where things are headed. We will address this further in chapter 10.

The Importance of Accountability

Coaching is an important job, and important jobs require accountability. A lack of accountability communicates that the job is unimportant. If each of your prospective coaches is responsible for two groups of approximately eight people, then they have sixteen people under their care as well as the eight or so people in their own group. Aren't twenty-five people worth looking after?

Over the years, I've discovered that new leaders who aren't supported by a coach have a harder time of actually starting a group. In the time between the new leader briefing and the start of the series, new leaders will face rejection, discouragement, and even outright spiritual attack. It's been my experience that more groups will stop before they actually start unless there is someone encouraging the leader. This is important work that deserves supervision.

If the expectation is for prospective coaches to call new leaders every week, then someone should follow up with the prospective coaches to make sure calls are being made. At a minimum level, prospective coaches are held accountable to fulfilling their commitments. But the more significant reasons are (1) the new leaders need the regular encouragement and direction so their groups will flourish, and (2) the small group pastor (and small group team in larger churches) needs to know what's going on with their groups.

Accountability Is Just a Simple Script

- Small group pastor asks prospective coaches what they are hearing from their group leaders.
- Prospective coaches either give an answer or confess they haven't made the calls.
- If negative response, then small group pastor says, "Well, why don't you call them over the next couple of days? Then I will give you a call at the end of the week." This gives them a deadline to make the calls.
- If positive response, then small group pastor says, "Thank you for following up with your leaders. I know they appreciate the encouragement. And thanks for letting me know how they're doing."

This is the opportunity for the small group pastor or team to address any issue the group leaders have that the prospective coach is not able to answer. This is really the genius of coaching: giving a personal response for every issue that group leaders face. If the coach can give the answer, then the small group pastor or team does not need to become involved or even informed. If the answer is beyond the coach, then only those issues come to the small group pastor or team.

Initially, supervising coaches can feel redundant. If a few coaches are calling a few group leaders and then the small group pastor has to call the coaches to make sure the calls are being made, couldn't the small group pastor just call the new leaders? The reality is that the small group pastor could call the new leaders, but over time the small group pastor would have too many direct reports. Later on, it's difficult to reassign leaders who report directly to the small group pastor to coaches. In fact, sometimes the small group pastor just has to live with it. But if the new leaders report to a coach from the beginning, even if it seems redundant, then as the small group ministry grows, the coaching structure will scale to meet demand. (See chapter 11 for a section on Coaching Reports.)

How to Evaluate Prospective Coaches

Once the series has concluded, it's time to assess how the prospective coaches performed in the execution of their responsibilities. Remember that the job description was simple:

- Make a weekly call to the new group leaders from the week of the briefing until the end of the series.
- Answer the new leaders' questions.
- Encourage the new leaders.
- Pray for the new leaders when you think of them.

Now for those who are supervising the prospective coaches, whether it's the small group pastor or small group team, there is probably already a pretty good sense of which prospective coaches have the stuff to become coaches and which do not. To verify how the prospective coaches feel about their experience, I've used a simple three-question survey like this:

1. How important do you feel your role was to the success of your leaders and groups?
2. How easy or difficult was it for you to contact your leaders?
3. How many of your groups are continuing?

Typically, this will line up on one side or the other. Some will report that they felt their role was important, that it was easy for them to contact their leaders, and that most (if not all) of their groups are continuing. These are the prospective coaches to invite into an on-going coaching relationship with these leaders, as well as a few more leaders in the future.

If the prospective coaches respond in the negative—they thought their role was unimportant, the leaders were difficult to contact, and most (if not all) of their groups are not continuing—then it's the end of the road on coaching. Simply conclude with thanking them for fulfilling their commitment and don't think twice. Since they agreed to help only in a temporary assignment, once the assignment is over, it's over.

This is the start of coaching, but there is far more to the coaching relationship. Coaching will change as group leaders grow personally and in their roles. Coaching will also take on disciple-making and spiritual formation aspects as the relationship develops. What started as instructional will transition to mentoring. These thoughts will be further developed in chapter 10.

Chapter 5

Recruiting Leaders

The method of recruiting leaders depends on how many new leaders the church needs and what they are willing to try. The church leadership must decide whether they want to increase the number of small groups incrementally or exponentially. There is not a right or a wrong here. It's just a matter of what goal the church is willing to pursue.

These strategies are based on my work with over fifteen hundred churches in North America. Of course, there are exceptions. For one, I've discovered that strategies that work well in other parts of the world don't always work so well when imported to North America.

Starting with No Groups

If the church doesn't have any groups, then how groups are started will have a bearing not only on the first group, but also on the coaching and support for future groups. The goal is not to start some groups just to have groups, but to begin with the end in mind and recruit your first group knowing you will need more group leaders and coaches as the small group ministry grows.

Start with one group that will be led by a pastor or someone with previous experience leading a group. The group members should be handpicked based on their ability or desire to eventually lead a group themselves. The purpose of this group is to model leading a group, while the members have a genuine group experience.

The group would meet for a designated period of time, which could be anywhere from six weeks to a semester or even up to a full year. The articulated expectation from the beginning should be for each group member to lead their own group upon graduation from this first group.

Once groups have started, this process could be repeated, or any of the following strategies could be implemented to recruit leaders and connect more people into groups. The church should never feel limited to use only one strategy to recruit leaders.

Connecting Up to 30 Percent in Groups

The first 30 percent of any congregation is the low-hanging fruit. These are the folks who are open to trying new things and who are loyal to the pastor and the church. These are easy yeses to get. There are three strategies commonly used in churches with 30 percent or fewer in groups.

1. Handpicking Leaders. In this method, the staff makes a list of people they know who meet the qualifications set by the church and would be good candidates for leading groups. Think about initially recruiting these leaders for a semester or up to a year. These new leaders would receive some sort of basic training that would include tasks such as gathering the group, preparing for the first meeting, facilitating a discussion, handing childcare, dealing with conflict, and other related topics. After these leaders complete the basic training, they should be released to start their groups. (For more on forming new groups, see chapter 7.)

Initially, I invited my leaders to fulfill either a one-year commitment or an indefinite commitment. Looking back, many of the people who eventually led groups using a different approach said no to a long commitment but accepted a shorter commitment initially, such as six weeks.

2. Apprenticing New Leaders and Multiplying Groups. In this approach, every small group leader recruits and mentors an apprentice leader in their group. At the appointed time, the group splits to form two groups. Either the existing leader leaves to form a new group and puts the new leader in charge or the new leader leaves to start a new group. In some scenarios, the existing leader and the new leader divide the group members between them and form two new groups.

After seven years of advocating this approach, only one group in our church in California actually did this. The rest either couldn't identify an apprentice or refused to leave their groups. You can read my full story in the introduction of *Exponential Groups*.

> *Key Factor to Connect 30 Percent: The small group pastor's relationship with the congregation and ability to motivate people to lead.*

Connecting 30 percent of a congregation is a tremendous achievement. Someone once told me that reaching this milestone places a church in the top one-half of one percent of all churches in North America. The other side of having 30 percent in groups is that this is a common place for small group ministries to get stuck. Both of the churches I served were stuck at 30 percent in groups at one point. In order to break beyond this barrier, the church must implement additional strategies. Please note these are "additional" strategies, not a replacement for what the church has built so far.

Over the years, I've seen too many pastors willing to wreck their churches over the newest, shiniest strategy out there. This is completely unnecessary and also not very smart. Allow what worked to connect the first 30 percent of the congregation to continue to work for them. This also applies to Sunday school, Bible studies, and other group formats. Then offer something new to the 70 percent of the congregation that effectively said no to what you were offering. Give them something they might say yes to.

Connecting Up to 60 Percent in Groups

While some churches have persisted at the previously described strategies and connected more than 30 percent into groups, this is not the case with most churches. Filling in the gap between 30 to 60 percent requires the addition of new strategies. Keep what was working, then offer additional options for those who rejected the initial offerings.

Both the handpicked strategy and the apprentice strategy faced certain limitations. The handpicked strategy was limited to the number of qualified candidates with whom the church staff was acquainted. At my church in California, this was certainly the case. Even though I had served the church for twelve years and watch the church grow from eighty-five adults to over eight hundred in worship, I reached a point where I had already tapped those I knew and the number of folks I didn't know was rapidly increasing. I needed a new way to identify potential leaders.

H.O.S.T. Home. This strategy was introduced by Saddleback Church in the first *40 Days of Purpose* church-wide campaign in 2002 (*EG* 12, 88–91). To increase the number of prospective group leaders in our church, some of the qualifications were set aside, such as those I personally knew, church membership, and extensive leadership training. These prospective leaders were qualified with an application (see page 74). Once they agreed to serve, we presented them to the congregation and offered a small group fair where prospective group members could sign up for the six week series.

In our first attempt at this strategy in 2004, we created a video-based curriculum based on our senior pastor's teaching, and our senior pastor became the spokesperson for leader recruitment. He stood up on a Sunday morning and made the invitation during his message: "We are starting a series on *The Passion of the Christ*. We have prepared materials based on my teaching. If you are willing to open your home to host one of these groups for the next six weeks, we'll help you get your group started." We doubled the number of leaders in one day. Now bear in mind, it had taken seven years of handpicking leaders to connect 30 percent of our adults in groups. I have not personally recruited a small group leader since 2004.

Training the Whole Group to Lead. Another issue came with our leaders being unable to identify apprentice leaders in their group. If they can't identify an apprentice, then you can't train one and they can't start a new group. I had pinned my hopes on the ability of my leaders to develop an apprentice, but they couldn't find any. As a workaround, I actually recruited prospective group leaders out of their groups for a training group and then released them to start groups. They were there in the groups. The leaders just couldn't see them. So we stopped doing that.

Picking up on a strategy developed by Brett Eastman and Lifetogether, we began to train the entire group instead of singling out one apprentice. The whole group became apprentices in a way. Everyone shared the responsibilities for the group meeting: bringing refreshments, hosting the group in their homes, leading the discussion or part of the discussion, planning a social event, leading an outreach project, leading the prayer time, and anything else the group leader could delegate. This worked best when the group leader made a request such as: "Everyone needs to take part in our group, so everyone needs to sign up to do something." (If the leader meekly asked if anyone would like to something, the answer more than likely would be no.) Then the leader needs to provide a simple sign-up sheet for group members to schedule when and how they will serve. It could look something like this:

Week	Lead Discussion	Part of Discussion	Host	Refreshments
1				
2				
3				
4				
5				
6				

Other group responsibilities can be assigned as they come up. If a particular group study calls for a group project or celebration event, then group members can be invited to join a team to plan for the event.

While sharing leadership solves part of the apprentice issue, it still leaves the issue open about group members not wanting to leave their groups to start new groups. The solution is in moving this issue from being the small group pastor's problem to being the group's problem. Groups that are good at inviting and including people should be encouraged to continue inviting new group members, even at the risk of overfilling their groups. When the group begins to feel uncomfortable about the number of people in their meeting location, then the coach or small group pastor should gently guide the group toward starting a new group. The conversation could go something like this:

> **Leader:** "Boy, we've had a packed house in our group meetings lately."
>
> **Coach:** "How are you handling that?"
>
> **Leader:** "Well, we crowd in to watch the teaching video, and then we break into subgroups for the discussion."
>
> **Coach:** "Who's leading the subgroup?"
>
> **Leader:** "Ben and Sue. They're doing a great job."
>
> **Coach:** "Well, keep me posted. It sounds like the way the group is growing that Ben and Sue might need to consider starting a new group."
>
> **Leader:** "You may be right."

Subgrouping is important for three reasons. First, it gives everyone a chance to get their word in during the discussion. Second, it gives an opportunity for group members to try their skills at leading the discussion. Third, it prepares the way for a new group to spin off of the current group.

Another consequence of overfilled groups is member attrition. Similar to worship services, once 80 percent of the room is filled, then it's full. Often when new people join a group and the space is tight, those new folks may not stick. This is only one reason. Other issues involve the group's openness to include new group members or the presence of an "EGR" (Extra Grace Required person!) in the group. All of these issues are coaching concerns that are valid to bring up in a coaching conversation.

> **Coach:** "I see that several new people came to your group for a while, but they're no longer attending."
>
> **Leader:** "Yes, a couple of them had schedule conflicts, but I'm not sure what happened to the other ones."
>
> **Coach:** "Is there anything going on in the group that might make them feel excluded or uncomfortable?"
>
> **Leader:** "Not really. Our group is very welcoming to new members and is careful about including them, even in side conversations. The only thing that might bother someone is that our group is averaging about sixteen people every week. We have to set up folding chairs, which aren't very comfortable. The room feels kind of crowded."
>
> **Coach:** "It sounds like that might be the issue. Do you feel there is someone in your group who might be ready to start a group with these new folks?"
>
> **Leader:** "Ben and Sue have been successfully leading part of the group for the discussion. I would hate to lose them, but they could certainly lead on their own."
>
> **Coach:** "Let's pray about this, then talk to them and see if they're open to that idea."

When multiplying groups is only the small group pastor's issue, the groups are not very motivated to change. But when groups need help dealing with too many members or members leaving, then they are more motivated to consider the option of starting a new group. There is one more strategy we will consider in the next section. If the group is preparing all of its members to lead, then the leader will have a better idea of who is interested in leading, who is able to lead, and who is ready to lead.

> *Key Factor to Connect 60 Percent: The senior pastor's leadership in recruiting group leaders, along with the small group pastor's ability to build a coaching structure and offer appropriate training.*

Connecting 100 Percent or More in Groups

While the HOST home strategy helped our church double our groups in a day, it also presented a limitation and a concern. The concern was that by promoting groups led by people we didn't know very well, the church was essentially endorsing that leader and group. This created an expectation in prospective group members that they were joining a group the church approved of, rather than joining a group led by someone the church really didn't know very well.

In the case of *The Passion of the Christ* series, our church worked hard to overcome being stuck at 30 percent in groups. Looking back, however, we should have vetted the leaders we presented a little more thoroughly and done something completely different with prospective leaders we didn't know very well or didn't know at all.

The limitation of the HOST home strategy is that it works only for people who are outgoing enough to welcome strangers into their homes, who are available during "normal" hours to host the group, and who are willing to participate in a program. In *Exponential Groups* (135–43), I write about these three groups: the Independents, the Introverts, and the Isolated. These three groups make up the last 30 percent of a congregation, who more than likely won't use any of the previously described methods of starting a group. Here's is how you can recruit them.

Start Your Own Group

Our team at New Life Christian Center in Turlock, California, was one of the first to pilot a "Grab and Go" strategy (*EG* 91–93). What we discovered was that starting your own group was far more popular than hosting a group or even joining a host home group. The invitation was simple: "Get together with your friends and do the study." We invited people to "lead" a "group" without using those words. This gave our people the permission and opportunity to start a group on their terms, one that worked for them. Whether they were introverts wanting to meet only with their close friends, or people with odd job schedules to work around, or families with special needs children who felt isolated, by giving them the ability to start a group that worked for them, our church ended up with more groups than we ever could have imagined. At New Life, we actually reached a place where we had a thousand adults in groups when we had only eight hundred adults in worship. We had connected 125 percent of our adults in groups. That's small potatoes, however, compared to a United Methodist Church in Georgia who connected five thousand people into groups with only twenty-five hundred in worship. The same was true of New Life Church in Renton, Washington, who launched four hundred additional groups to connect five thousand in groups.

Then there was Kingdom Life Church in Baltimore, Maryland, led by Pastor Michael Phillips. With their self-produced series *Back to Church*, this congregation with six hundred in Sunday worship started a hundred sixty-seven groups for their series. If you do the math, they didn't need a hundred sixty-seven leaders times ten members each to start of these groups. They needed only a hundred sixty-seven people willing to gather a group of friends to start a group.

The key to launching groups this way is to put the responsibility of forming the group on the person who starts the group (more on this in chapter 7). To make this a better experience for the group members and the church, these groups should not be advertised. Designate these groups as "Invitation Only," meaning that the leader is inviting 100 percent of the group members, but don't list the groups on the church website, a group directory, or at a connection event or small group fair. Don't send prospective members to these groups. If new groups want to be open to new members, like a host home, then the leaders should be more thoroughly vetted or interviewed as described in chapter 3.

Small Group Vacation

Simply put, members of established small groups all leave the group during an alignment series or semester to start new groups. Since groups have shared responsibilities with their group members, the members should have developed some leadership skills and experience facilitating discussions. This is a great way to kick these potential leaders out of the nest and start new groups.

The invitation from the senior pastor goes like this: "Some of you have been in a group for a long time. For this next series/semester, we want you to temporarily leave your current group to help us start some new groups. After the series is over, you can go back to the group you were in before." The small group pastor should give the established group leaders a heads-up before this announcement is made, but the senior pastor should be the one who broaches the subject with the group members during a worship service and also via e-mail. Small group leaders should be encouraged to encourage their members to sign on for this.

What usually happens is that about 80 percent of the group members who start a group will stay with the new group after the series ends. Some may try to lead a group and rejoin their previous group, but after a while they won't be able to continue to do both.

This is also a great way to breathe new life into established groups whose attendance has dwindled over time. Unless the group is really good at welcoming and including new members, new people will have a hard time joining the group and feeling comfortable. This doesn't mean they're a bad group. It just means that over time they have become a close-knit family, which is what we want, right? The problem is that it is hard for new people to stick to close-knit groups. By encouraging the members of established groups to take a vacation and start new groups during an alignment series or semester, the leaders of the established group can refill the group with all new group members. Even if some of the established members come back to the group, they will more likely stick because they've had six weeks or so together as a new group.

> ***Key Factor for Connecting over 100 Percent:** The senior pastor gives permission and opportunity for church members and attendees to start groups on their terms.*

▶ Case Study ◀

Hoboken Grace Church

Hoboken Grace is a church of eight hundred adults in Hoboken, New Jersey, near New York City. This region is known for young, single, upwardly mobile residents who eventually marry and move to the suburbs. The church is eleven years old and has offered small groups since its beginning.

The church's effort at groups had connected about five hundred of their eight hundred members into groups. But the operative word here is *effort*. "At that point, identifying new group leaders was heavy apprenticing and heavy individual recruiting," said Nick Lenzi, the church's community director. "We had a reluctance to church-wide campaigns. We felt it was really hard to create our own curriculum, or at least we thought the barriers for that were really high."

For their first church-wide campaign, the church chose to purchase curriculum for their *Be Rich* series. The topic was finances, and the curriculum choice was from Dave Ramsey's Financial Peace University (FPU). This was the direction the lead pastor was going in their sermon series, so the small group campaign followed suit.

What's more, FPU required the facilitators to have advanced training. Nine months before the campaign, the church let the group leaders know about the series. "In January, we had the pastor put together a vision video," Lenzi said. "He told them, 'I want you guys to get into FPU because we need as many qualified people this fall to take the entire church through FPU. If you know the material, you're going to have a huge leg up and be able to help so many people.' When our people heard from the lead pastor, they accepted that call to action."

"We were starting community and talking about the most intimate thing in today's society," Lenzi admits. Yet, in this first alignment series, the church was able to connect 91 percent of their adults into groups. They had connected an additional 28 percent of their adults into groups using a relatively difficult topic.

With one series under their belt, the church took the next step to create their own teaching videos to align with a published series (with permission). "I got a teleprompter," Lenzi said. "My pastor asked, 'Where has this thing been my whole life?'"

The church also decided to try a new strategy in recruiting group leaders. "One of our values is that everyone in the church takes responsibility for their own spiritual growth. Now I'm looking for leaders who are able to encourage a group and support people in their own spiritual growth. When we invite people to lead groups, we invite them to encourage people and help these gatherings to happen. The church is going to partner with them. We're going to give them the questions. We're going to offer the video teaching. We'll put the leaders in touch with the care pastors if something comes up. This has been so fruitful. My 'close rate' is 90 to 95 percent, because everyone believes they can encourage someone else. The nature of the groups is going from house to house, or restaurant to restaurant. We've found that we just need to get out of the way and let the Holy Spirit be the Holy Spirit."

With their pastor's video teaching and an openness to give their people permission and opportunity to lead these gatherings, Hoboken Grace continues to make a kingdom impact in a neighborhood of the biggest city in the United States.

Sample Scripts for Recruiting Group Leaders for the Senior Pastor

> **Six Weeks Prior to the Launch. Message to Existing Group Leaders (include series "Trailer, an overview video of the teaching series")**

- Thanks for leading.
- I want to give you the first look at our upcoming series
- I need your help:
  - There's an opportunity for hundreds of new people to gather their friends and grow.
  - I know this is not the way you came into group life.
  - This is a little risky. Might be messy. This is why I need you.
  - Would you walk alongside a couple of these new hosts for one study, just for six weeks?
  - Could you call them once per week, answer their questions, pray for them?
  - When it's all said and done, the new hosts will have the same training and coaching opportunities you have had.
  - Please reply to this e-mail to let me and [contact] know you can help us during this series.

> **Sample Script for Existing Group Leaders**

"As your pastor I want to thank you for serving your small group. Our church believes that small groups are essential to the life and ministry of our church. Your group is providing care and spurring on growth in profound ways. I know I'm preaching to the choir, but I want you to know that I believe in what you're doing, and I'm grateful for what you do.

"This [season] we are offering a church-wide series to help other people find the community that you enjoy in your small group. Watch the series trailer in this e-mail to get a sense of where we're headed. This series might be a good fit for your group, but if it's not I understand. We're all in different places in our spiritual growth. But there are a couple of things I hope you would consider.

"First, since we are recruiting new leaders for this series, we need your help. Our current coaching structure will be completely overloaded. We need you to walk alongside one or two of these new leaders during the series to encourage them, answer their questions, and pray for them. If you will help us, please click the link below.

"Second, there may be a few folks in your group who could lead one of these groups. Encourage them to take their next step in leading their own group for this series. And as a bonus, when they start their group, you get to be their coach.

"And last, as we are gearing up for this series, please be in prayer for the new leaders and group members as well as our staff team and pastors.

"Thanks for giving me a few minutes of your time."

Five Weeks Prior to the Launch

Message to Core Church Members (include "Trailer" of series)

- Importance of groups at [our church].
- What [the series topic] means to [senior pastor] and could mean to them.
- "I want everybody in this thing."
- In next couple weeks, you will be hearing more about the series.
- Please respond and let me know if I can count on you to host a group.

Sample Script to Core Church Members

"I'm excited about the upcoming series, [Title]. I believe you will benefit greatly by participating in this series. I also believe this is a topic that will interest a lot of people both in our church and in our neighborhoods.

"I want to challenge you with something. When you think of [Topic], who in your life comes to mind? Who would benefit from a series like this? When you think about your friends, neighbors, coworkers, family members, and others, who needs something like this right now? I want to challenge you to gather the people you know and do this study together. If you're currently in a small group, I want you to step outside of that group just for the six weeks of this series to do this study with your friends. Your current small group leader will be available to coach you. We'll provide everything you need. The study is based on my teaching on video, so you don't need to be the teacher or the Bible expert. That's my part. You just watch the video with your friends and then ask the questions in the discussion guide. That's not too difficult.

"Can I count on you to gather a group and grow together this [season]? If you'll do it, please click the link below and let me know that you're in. Thanks for your time. This is going to be a great season for our church."

Four Weeks Prior to the Launch

Promotional Video in the Worship Service: Series Trailer

- [Something about the series to clarify.]
- Will you join me?
- This promo is specific to the topic of the series and why the pastor is excited about it.

Three Weeks Prior to the Launch

Promotional Video in the Worship Service: Why Groups?

- Why [senior pastor] is passionate about groups.
- The video curriculum is easy for anyone to start a group.
- Best part: gather with your friends, not a bunch of strangers.
- Five or six people, not ten or twelve.

Sample Script for Recruiting Host Homes

"You're heard me talk about the series we've put together for this [season]. I want you to be a part of this by opening your home and inviting a few people to do this study with you. Think about your friends, family, coworkers, neighbors, or others who would enjoy or benefit from this study. A name probably just came to mind. Invite them to join you. This study is so easy to do. The teaching is on video, so you don't need to worry about being a teacher or a Bible expert. You and your group will watch the video together and then answer some questions about what it means to you and how you can live it out.

"I realize that in a church our size, there are some people who don't know very many people yet. After you have a few of your friends in the group, then you'll also have an opportunity to meet some prospective group members and add them to your group as well. You'll find out more at the briefing.

"What do you think? Can I count on you to host a group this [season]?"

Then go into the method of collecting the response with a sign-up card, text message, or online survey. See page 63 of this workbook for more information.

Two Weeks Prior to the Launch

Promotional Video in the Worship Service: What Are You Waiting for?

- Either the third time is the charm or three strikes you're out, right?
- You can do this study with your family, with a couple of friends, with a disillusioned coworker, or with a neighbor.
- Jesus said where two or three are gathered; I would have to agree with that.

Sample Script for Recruiting People to Gather Their Friends for the Study

On the weekend prior to the series launch, the church can do a couple of things:

- Offer a connection event or small group fair for people to sign up for groups (see the details in chapter 7).
- Ask the groups to host an open house with their new group members. The following is an outline for a video from the senior pastor that could be shown at the open house welcoming everyone to the series.

Optional: One Week Prior to the Launch

Series Video Introduction from the Senior Pastor for Group Open House Week

- Thank you for joining together for the series
- How [the series] came about
- From the heart: what [senior pastor] really hopes they take away from this series
- Contact info: small group calendar
- Shared responsibilities: small group calendar; sign up for something today

Making the Actual Invitation for New Leaders

I want to spend a little time here walking through the actual steps to secure the response from those who want to lead a group, host a group, or do the study with their friends. This may appear to be simple, but the timing and the nuance is significant. *Exponential Groups* gives some additional content on connecting the invitation and the response (see *EG* 97–100).

During the service, the senior pastor should make an appeal for group leaders (or whatever strategy you are using that week). The invitation can be made before, during, or after the sermon. In the case of a sermon in this chapter by Dr. Tony Evans, the entire sermon was an invitation that netted two hundred seventy responses to host a group. If the invitation to lead a group is made before or in the middle of the sermon, then it's important to remind the congregation to respond at the end of the sermon as well.

I also recommend sending a version of the same invitation to church members via e-mail the following week. Again, keeping the response time close to the invitation, the e-mail should have a prominent button for prospective leaders to click and sign up to lead.

The Collection Tool

The response must be collected while the congregation is still in the room. Once the congregation leaves, chances are slim they will remember to sign up. To collect the response, a tool must be available in the worship service for people to easily respond to the invitation to lead a group. Whether the tool is a sign-up card or a digital solution, the key is to offer something that is easy to use and allows for an immediate response.

The prospective leader only needs to provide their essential contact information: Name, e-mail address, and cell phone number. Then they need to commit to attend a briefing, which should occur either that day or the next weekend. Even if the church is providing additional briefings (I recommend a briefing after every worship service for three weeks in a row), list only the next two briefings on the sign-up card or online form.

The card could look like this example from Calvary Christian Church in Winchester, Kentucky:

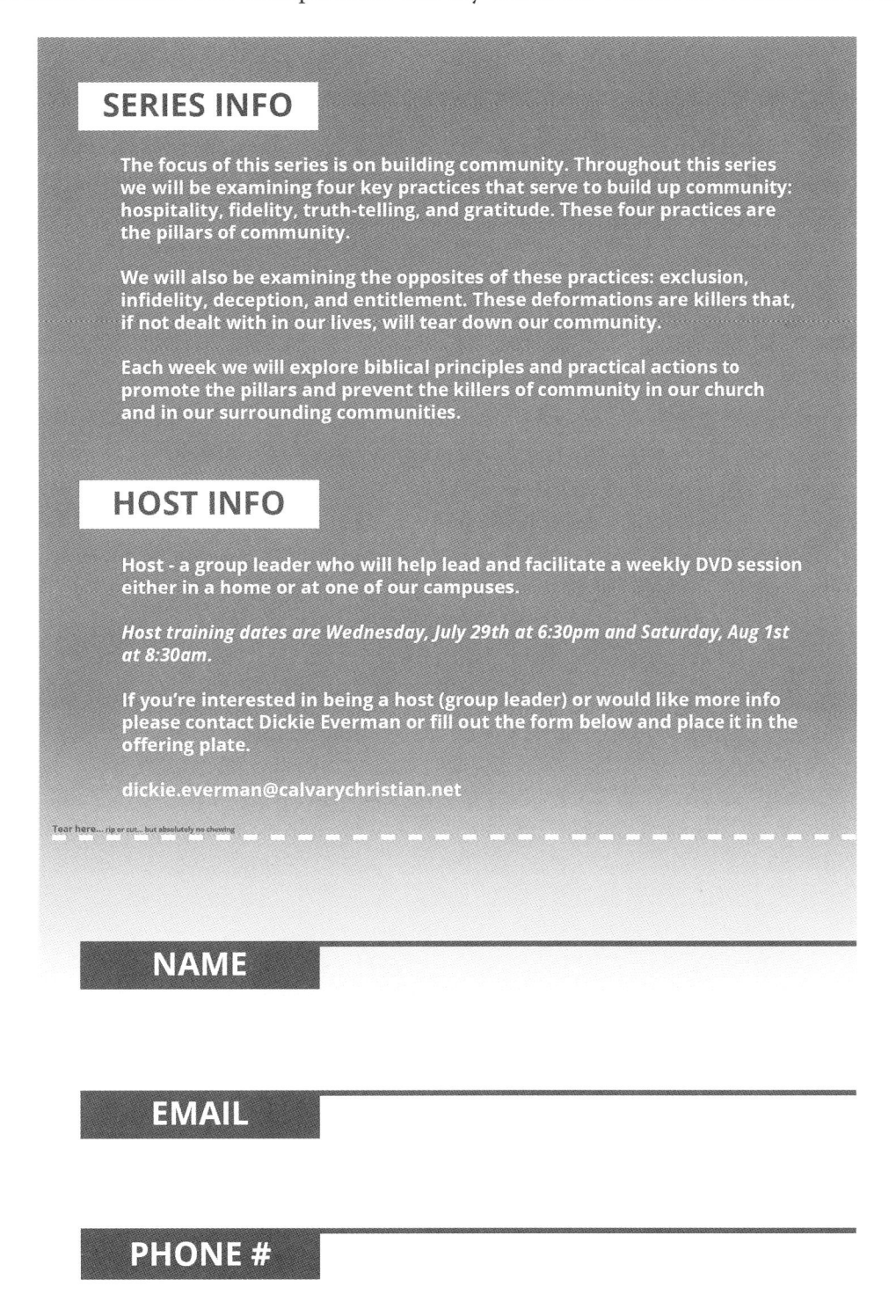

SERIES INFO

The focus of this series is on building community. Throughout this series we will be examining four key practices that serve to build up community: hospitality, fidelity, truth-telling, and gratitude. These four practices are the pillars of community.

We will also be examining the opposites of these practices: exclusion, infidelity, deception, and entitlement. These deformations are killers that, if not dealt with in our lives, will tear down our community.

Each week we will explore biblical principles and practical actions to promote the pillars and prevent the killers of community in our church and in our surrounding communities.

HOST INFO

Host - a group leader who will help lead and facilitate a weekly DVD session either in a home or at one of our campuses.

Host training dates are Wednesday, July 29th at 6:30pm and Saturday, Aug 1st at 8:30am.

If you're interested in being a host (group leader) or would like more info please contact Dickie Everman or fill out the form below and place it in the offering plate.

dickie.everman@calvarychristian.net

Tear here... rip or cut... but absolutely no chewing

- -

NAME

EMAIL

PHONE #

Even if prospective leaders will attend a briefing that day, they still need to fill out a card or register online. There is something significant about "signing on the dotted line" as a commitment to the pastor's invitation.

If the church is using a physical card, then the card should be placed in the offering basket, handed to an usher, or otherwise collected in the service. Once a commitment card leaves the room, you will never see it again.

Sample Video Scripts to Promote an Alignment Series and Cast Vision for Groups

These promo videos were used prior to recruiting leaders to promote the series in the pastor's absence. Videos like these can also be used to promote an alignment series by e-mail or through social media.

Beatitudes Promo Script by Scott McKee, Senior Pastor
Ward Church, Northville, Michigan

Promo #1

"I want to invite you to join me this fall for an inside look at the upside-down kingdom. In just a few paragraphs, Jesus of Nazareth paints an unforgettable picture of the blessed life. We call these statements the Beatitudes, and they are the counterintuitive keys to happiness. These statements take a little time to absorb. They are unexpected and unsettling. Studying the beatitudes is best done with a group of friends. We can help each other probe their depths and apply their insights. Make plans to start a group or join a group for this eight-session look at the words of Jesus. The life Jesus calls us to is not easy, but it is blessed. See you soon."

Promo #2

"Hey, everybody, I am here in this beautiful high-rise apartment overlooking the City of Detroit, where we have just recorded the video lessons for our upcoming small group series on the Beatitudes of Jesus. The city skyline provides the perfect setting for a discussion of the upside-down kingdom of God. So get some friends together and join us for this eight-week exploration of the wisest teaching ever given. If you have been waiting for the right time to start a group or join a group, this is it! There is no better time than this fall, this series, this topic. We are going to learn together about the blessed life. Join us."

Promo #3

"I am in this beautiful high-rise apartment overlooking the Detroit River and the city landscape on a spectacular and sunny day. We have just completed shooting the videos for our fall small group curriculum, which—if I may say so—is going to be outstanding. Of course, we have great source material. We are going to be studying some of the most countercultural statements in human history. They were spoken by Jesus of Nazareth on a mountain about two thousand years ago. The Beatitudes, as we refer to these statements today, form the introduction to the famous Sermon on the Mount. It will be our privilege to explore these statements together.

"I wanted to record the videos here in this location for several reasons. First of all, I wanted a beautiful setting to form a visually stimulating backdrop. Second, I wanted a city setting as a symbol of humility now bearing greatness, an ideal place to talk about the upside-down kingdom. But third and most importantly, I wanted to shoot the videos in a place that was free! Some friends loaned me the use of their apartment to shoot these videos. They don't actually know about it. They are on vacation. But I think they would be honored that someone used the key under their doormat for such a noble project. I hope you will pull together some friends in your apartment or house and join me for this important study of the blessed life."

Promo #4 for Small Group Leaders

"Hey, small group leaders, I want to personally thank you for your work leading a Ward Church small group. I really believe that a small intentional community of friends is the best environment to live and love like Jesus. Sunday morning sermons are important, right? Somebody? Anybody? Sermons are important, but it is discussion in small settings that drives the learning home and helps us to put our learning into practice. This fall, I am asking you to partner with me again for a sermon-based small-group series on the Beatitudes of Jesus. I will give a Sunday sermon on one of the Beatitudes, and then you will lead a discussion on that same theme in your small group. And we will continue that lecture/lab rhythm for eight weeks. The Beatitudes are so rich, so countercultural, so potentially life-altering that I don't want to rush through them.

"I will provide a short video for you to show to your group each week to get the conversation going. The videos have been recorded right here overlooking the beautiful Detroit skyline. I chose to shoot the videos here because of the beauty and life in Detroit that defies its often negative stereotype. Things are not always what they seem. In this study, we will learn from Jesus about the upside-down kingdom of God, about the inversion of values from God's perspective, and about what it really means to be blessed.

"I am looking forward to exploring the wisdom of Jesus together with you. Please mark your calendars and organize your group members for this study. It all begins the week of September 29. Thank you and God bless."

Chapter 6

Initial Training

Exponential Groups (103–20) provides a great deal of detail on the subject of the new leader briefing. I believe that the training of leaders is so important that I spend a full hour with my coaching groups to cover all of the rationale and mechanics of a fifteen-minute briefing of these new leaders. It's as important to know what to cover as it is to know what not to cover in a briefing. We want to give prospective leaders enough information to get started, but without overwhelming them with every possible issue that could come up in their groups. I've found that too much training can actually end up talking new leaders out of leading a group! It's better to allow an experienced leader or coach to walk the new leader through these issues when an issue arises in their group rather than over-train at the beginning. Here's a list of what I believe are essentials to discuss in that fifteen minutes to help them get started:

- Provide the logistics of the study: where, when, what, etc.
- Explain how they can go about putting together a group
- Explain how they should share leadership roles in their group
- Finally, introduce these new leaders to their coaches

Other issues—such as childcare, leading their first meeting, keeping the discussion on track, reporting attendance, and so on—can be addressed in a briefing packet that they can read later. Briefings should be brief! If the new leaders have questions beyond what the packet addresses, then they can talk to their coaches.

Sample Briefing Agenda and Presentation

Briefing Agenda

- Senior pastor welcomes new leaders.
- Small group pastor (SGP) welcomes everyone.
- SGP covers series logistics, gathering a group, and sharing leadership.
- SGP introduces the coaches/experienced leaders.
- Coaches/experienced leaders partner with new leaders and exchange contact information.
- New leaders complete the Information Sheet.
- Curriculum is distributed to those who turn in their Information Sheets.
- Briefing ends.

Briefing Presentation

Living a Balanced Life

NEW LEADER BRIEFING PRESENTATION

Series Details

- SIX WEEKS: [INSERT DATES]
- WEEKLY MESSAGES FROM OUR PASTOR
- STUDY GUIDE BY ALLEN WHITE
- WEEKLY VIDEO-BASED SMALL GROUP STUDY

When, Where, How . . .

- THE GROUPS WILL MEET WEEKLY FOR 1.5 TO 2 HOURS
- DAY: HOST WILL CHOOSE
- TIME: HOST WILL CHOOSE
- LOCATION: OFF-CAMPUS
- LENGTH OF COMMITMENT: SIX WEEKS
- REFRESHMENTS: WHATEVER YOUR GROUP CHOOSES!

Build Your Group

- INVITE YOUR FRIENDS
- USE THE SMALL GROUP POSTCARDS
- CONNECT AT SMALL GROUP CONNECTIONS: AFTER SERVICE ON SUNDAYS, [INSERT DATES]
- USE THE CHURCH WEBSITE

A Coach in Your Corner

- AN EXPERIENCED LEADER OR COACH WILL GUIDE YOU
- CALL THEM BACK!
- ASK THEM QUESTIONS
- REMEMBER, THEY ARE PRAYING FOR YOU!

Sample Briefing Packet from Brookwood Church, Simpsonville, South Carolina

Living a Balanced Life: New Leader Briefing

Series Overview

Most of us are balancing more than two things. When we go from two objects to three objects or more, we have suddenly gone from balancing to juggling. Isn't that how we feel? Every day we have to keep a certain number of balls up in the air or plates spinning. If we drop a ball, then it seems like the whole thing will come crashing down.

The Bible tells us in Luke 2:52 that "Jesus grew in wisdom and in stature and in favor with God and all the people" (NLT). Working from this passage, we are going to examine four major areas of our lives: our relationship with God, our relationship with others, our physical health, and our wisdom capacity. For the first five lessons, we will examine a passage of Scripture, and then take an assessment to see where and how we need to grow. In the final lesson, we will create an action plan for tackling one of these growth areas.

Series Components

- Weekly message series taught by our pastors (September 20–October 18)
- *Living a Balanced Life Small Group Study Guide* by Allen White
- Six-session small group DVD

Living a Balanced Life Timeline

August 30–September 7	New Leader Briefings
	Start Inviting Your Group Members
August 30	Small Group Leadership Training I
September 13 and 20	Small Group Connection
September 20	Series Starts
	Week of First Group Meeting
	Lesson 1: Our Need for Balance
September 27	Lesson 2: Finding Favor with God
October 4	Lesson 3: Finding Favor with People
October 11	Lesson 4: Living a Healthy Lifestyle
October 18	Lesson 5: Gaining Wisdom
October 25	Lesson 6: Taking Action

Getting Started

- When will groups meet? September 20–October 25 (day of the week is your choice).
- How often will groups meet? Weekly for 6 weeks.
- How long are the meetings? Allow 1½ hours, plus about 30 minutes for socializing afterward.
- What is the commitment? 6 weeks.
- What do I need for the first night? A clean house, a "reviewed" lesson, and some snacks and drinks.
- Who will help me if I have a problem? Your coach.

Gathering Your Group

How People Can Join Your Group

1. Personal Invitation
Use the "Circles of Life," your "speed dial" list, your Christmas card list; who in your life would *enjoy* or *benefit* from this study?

2. Church Website
Log on today and setup your group. (See instructions for creating your group in the church's online database.) [NB: This information is not included in the *Exponential Groups Workbook*.]

3. Small Group Connection
On Sundays, September 13 and 20, small groups that are doing the *Living a Balanced Life* study will participate in the Small Group Connection between each service. It's simple: You just stand near a banner for your town or your affinity (men, women, couples, singles, parents, etc.) and meet folks who want to join a group for *Living a Balanced Life*.

The Basics

Co-host: You need a co-host, because you will need a break! Think of someone (whom you like!) and invite them to join you as the co-host. There may be someone who signs up who can fit this role. Don't do this alone!

Childcare: The easier the childcare, the easier it is for people to join your group. Consider some childcare options: Does someone from the church live nearby? Do you know a member of the youth group or someone else who could help? Don't stress on this one: *Pray!*

Group Format and Curriculum: The group discussion will be directed by the teaching video. You might want to watch the video ahead of time to prepare yourself, but the video will do most of the work for you. Follow the instructions in the study guide. Start with the "Connect" section, view the teaching video when directed, and then continue with the discussion questions.

Rotate the Responsibilities. There is no reason that you have to do everything for your group. On the first night of the study, challenge *everyone* to take a part: volunteer to bring refreshments, open their home, or lead the discussion. Use the group calendar on page 66 of the study guide to schedule everyone.

Remember that it is *God* alone who has assembled your group and given you the opportunity to lead; and without question, it is *God* who will supply the grace and the strength to guide you and your group through this series.

Helpful Suggestions for Group Leaders

Suggestions to Assist You As You Lead Your Group:

God is in charge. Rely solely on him and be faithful in prayer for strength and wisdom. You were not selected to do this on your own, nor were you selected to serve without being served. Be open and willing for how God wants to use you to lead while he alone does his work in you.

Partner Up. Partner with a spouse, a friend, or another group member for prayer support, as well as practical assistance in hospitality, follow up, and reporting.

Be Prepared. Be prepared to review and discuss the sessions before your group arrives. Simply review the DVD session and small group chapters in advance.

Be Open. God wants to use you as you are—where you are in your own journey to connect with those in your group. Most importantly, as a group, support each other in prayer while ensuring a safe harbor of confidentiality. Honor each other by listening, encouraging, praying, and keeping confidentiality as a nonnegotiable principle.

Encourage Participation. While each of us is wired differently, it is important to orchestrate conversation that encourages each type of personality to feel comfortable over time.

Have Fun. This is not a task on your to-do list. This is God at work through your willingness to lead. Often groups begin with dinner where social connection becomes a key ingredient to trusting each other and growing together.

Ask for Input. Be flexible on how you lead and how the group wishes to refine the amount of time spent and the flow of the session. There is not one perfect way.

Pray. Pray often and pray consistently and in cooperation with reading the Bible daily. Your strength and sustenance will come from reading and seeking God in prayer. Surrender in advance to your own ideas and agendas and replace them with inviting God to lead you and your group.

Keys to a Successful Group

Keeping Your Meeting On Track

It's easy to chase rabbit trails. So if you feel like your group is starting on a subject outside of the curriculum, just say something like, "Well, that's going to open a whole other can of worms; let's go to the next question," or "Well, guys, that's going to be a whole other (day, show, discussion); let's get back to today's discussion." Don't interrupt people. When you find the opportunity, get it back on track.

If the discussion turns to criticism, please ask the critical person to go and speak directly to the person responsible. They would love to talk with them about their concern.

If something comes up that you don't know how to answer or deal with, just be honest. "I'm not sure about that one. Can I get back to you next week?"

Don't Walk Alone

All of the new hosts will have a coach to answer your questions and help you start you group. Your coach will call you regularly to see how you're doing. Most importantly, your coach and their small group will be praying for you.

If you are currently in a small group, then your coach can be your small group leader.

If you're not in a small group, then you'll meet a coach *today* who will help you get your group started.

Reporting Your Group's Progress

Check in with your coach at least once per week.

Report online attendance, prayer requests, and other needs. [Add your church's website information and reporting procedure.]

We would also like to know what's happening in your group: decisions for Christ, answers to prayer, life changes, and so on.

Childcare Options

Note: The harder it is for new members to arrange childcare, the less likely they will join the group.

- Recruit someone to do children's ministry while your group is meeting.
- Hire a babysitter. Have each member chip in.
- Allow older children to supervise younger children, with adults checking in.
- Ask group members to trade off in watching the children each week.
- Allow the children to take part in the group. Offer topics and activities where everyone can participate.
- Have each member arrange for their own childcare.

Small Group Connection: September 13 & 20

Connection Overview

This is an opportunity for folks at Brookwood to meet you face-to-face and sign up for your Living a Balanced Life Small Group. The connection will take place after each of the three Sunday morning services, so plan on being here on September 13 and 20. Remember that more people come to the first and second services. You will get the most signups after the third service.

Connection Process

1. Meet at 9:30 a.m. in the Concourse for last minute instructions and prayer.

2. Stand near the sign for your city or affinity (men, women, couples, singles, parents, etc.).

3. Meet the other hosts standing nearby. You might be able to direct someone to their group as well.

4. Meet folks as they leave the auditorium. Tell them a little bit about your group. Invite them to your group.

5. If they are interested, sign them up on the spot and give them your group handout. You need to collect their name, email address, and preferred phone number.

6. At the end of the Connection, turn in one copy of your group roster to Small Group Solutions and keep one copy for yourself.

After the Connection

1. Call your new group members and remind them of the first meeting. You might even ask someone to bring a snack. (This is great, especially if they're sitting on the fence: "Well, I'm not sure if we can make it." Then, you say: "Shoot, I was hoping you could bring a snack for the group . . .")

2. Add your new group members to your group on the Small Groups website.

3. Pray for God's blessing on your first meeting.

4. Connect with your coach.

Your First Meeting

Welcome each of your group members and introduce them to other members if they are new. Offer them a beverage. Sometimes a small cup offers a little security for first timers. If they don't want to respond, they can just take a drink.

If your group has been together for a while or several group members know each other really well, it is especially important that you make every effort to help new folks feel included.

Avoid grouping up with your buddies. If something comes up in conversation that is an inside joke or story, please take extra time to explain the background to your new members so they'll feel included.

The first night sets the tone for your group. It doesn't need to be perfect, but it does need to be warm and friendly. Here are a couple of suggestions:

1. Introduce yourselves and talk about where you grew up. Name tags might help on the first night.

2. Allow others plenty of time to think about their answers and respond. If you find yourself talking too much, count to ten before you answer.

At the end of the evening, remind everyone of when and where you'll meet next and thank them for coming. Even if you have to break away from another conversation, don't let new members leave without a goodbye from you.

Sample Phone Script 1: Calling those who have requested a group

Here are some important points to cover in your call:

- Introduce yourself by name from _____ Church. Ask if they have a moment to talk.
- Indicate that you are a Group Host and would like to invite them to participate in a small group/Bible study experience in your home on (the day of the week you have selected) at (the time you have selected).
- If they plan to attend, provide your telephone number and address with directions to your home. Reconfirm the date and time.
- End with an inviting closing such as "Can't wait to have you in my home" or "I'm looking forward to you joining us."

Sample Phone Script 2: Visiting/Calling a Neighbor

Points to cover in your contact:

- Introduce yourself as their neighbor on_____ [your street name].
- Indicate that you are planning to have a group of neighbors meet at your home on [day of the week and time] for a six-week study about *Living a Balanced Life*.
- Ask them if they would like to come check it out. (If they want to know more, tell them that your group is doing a new study to go along with our series *Living a Balanced Life*.)
- If Yes: Provide your telephone number and address with directions to your home. Reconfirm the date and time.
- If No: Thank them and offer your telephone number in case they change their mind.
- End with an inviting closing such as, "Can't wait to have you in my home," or, "I'm looking forward to you joining us." Or "Please feel free to come if you change your mind."

[Church Database Information can be added to the briefing packet so the new leaders will know how to set up their groups, update their rosters, and take attendance.]

New Leader Information

My Group is:
- ☐ Open to New Members
- ☐ "Invitation Only" Group

Coach: _____
This is either your current small group leader or the coach you meet in this briefing today

Name: _____ Spouse: _____

Address: _____

City: _____ Zip: _____

Home Phone: _____ Cell Phone: _____

E-mail: _____

Group Meeting Specifics:

    Day of the Week: _____ Time of Day: _____ AM or PM

    Location of Meeting (subdivision, if applicable): _____

    Address: _____

    Type of Group: Anybody   Couples   Singles   Women only   Men only

    Childcare available: Yes   No

How and when did you commit your life to Jesus Christ?

How long have you attended our church? Where did you attend church before?

Why do you want to host a small group? (You don't have to make this overly spiritual or complicated!)

Is there anything going on in your life that could potentially harm or embarrass the church?

Current habitual struggles or moral issues (addiction, cohabitation, sexual relationship outside of marriage, or similar) that would bring shame on the name of Jesus Christ or on our church.

Current marital struggles (infidelity, separation, divorce in process, or similar)

Here is another example of the new leader application from Justin Ristow, Small Group Pastor, Olive Branch Community Church, Corona, California.

INVITE ONLY Group Registration
[year] Campaign Edition
Name(s):_____ **Today's date:**_____

Best number to reach you: _____

Best time to normally reach you during the week (Mon–Fri)?

- In the morning between _____ **a.m.** and _____ **a.m.**
- In the afternoon or evening between _____ **p.m.** and _____ **p.m.**

E-mail: _____

Age: ☐ 18–25   ☐ 26–35   ☐ 36–45   ☐ 46–60   ☐ 61+

Marital Status: ☐ Single   ☐ Married   ☐ Other

How long have you been attending our church? _____

When did you come to faith? _____

Have you been a part of a small group before?   ☐ Yes   ☐ No

What night will your group meet on?

☐ Mon   ☐ Tues   ☐ Wed   ☐ Thurs   ☐ Fri   ☐ Sat   ☐ Sun

What time do you think your group will begin?

☐ 6:00 p.m.   ☐ 7:00 p.m.   ☐ Other (specify):_____

What type of group would you like to start?

☐ Anyone (Couples & Singles)   ☐ Couples   ☐ Men's   ☐ Women's   ☐ Singles

Where is the group planning to meet?

☐ My home   ☐ Another member's home (name):_____

City:_____ Nearest cross streets:_____

If you already know whom you're planning to invite to your group, please list their names below (use back if you need more space):

1. _____   4. _____

2. _____   5. _____

3. _____   6. _____

Would you be open to other people from our church joining your group?

If yes, please answer the questions on back

☐ No, this is an invite only group for now   ☐ Yes, 7+   ☐ Yes, 4–6   ☐ Yes, 1–3

Please answer questions below only if you want other people from our church to join your group

Have you taken the church membership class?   ☐ Yes   ☐ No

Do you believe the Bible is the ultimate authority for your life?   ☐ Yes   ☐ No

Do you believe that you have the time, emotional capacity, and moral discernment to lead a group?   ☐ Yes   ☐ No

Leader must not have current habitual struggles or moral issues (drugs, alcohol, cohabitation, etc.) that would bring shame on the name of Jesus Christ or on our church. In addition, there must not be any current serious marital struggles (e.g., infidelity, separation, divorce in process, etc.).

FOR OFFICE USE ONLY:

Curriculum Picked Up:

Date Picked Up	Leader Guide	DVD	Participant Guides

Coach Assigned: _____

Service Attended: ☐ Sat 5:00 p.m.   ☐ Sun 8:00 a.m.   ☐ Sun 9:30 a.m.   ☐ Sun 11:00 a.m.

Briefing Sign-In Sheet

If preregistered, please put name and check column 2 only.

Name	Preregistered?	E-mail	Cell Phone

Briefing Checklist

- ☐ Invite senior pastor to welcome new leaders
- ☐ Presentation slides
- ☐ Projector and screen
- ☐ Copies of Briefing Packet
- ☐ New Leader Information sheet (two-part form: coach copy and church copy)
- ☐ Briefing Sign-In Sheet
- ☐ Pens
- ☐ Coaches scheduled to meet new leaders
- ☐ Curriculum: study guides for distribution and video access or DVDs

Chapter 7

Connection Strategy

I've seen churches get everything I've talked about so far exactly right and then completely blow it when it comes to forming groups. Their senior pastor is onboard with casting vision for groups and even creating a series. They have recruited leaders. Coaches are in place to support the groups. Everything is ready to go, but how they choose to fill the groups will determine the success of these groups. The temptation in a church of any size is to use task-oriented approaches like sign-up cards, the church website or app, or small group directories to connect people into groups. Just pick a group, any group, and it will work out, right? Wrong!

To sign up for a group in the church my family attends, prospective group members go to a bank of computers in the church's "Next Step" area, then search the group directory on the church's website. In a conversation with the campus small group pastor at the church's original campus, the success rate of this approach came to light.

Me: How many people signed up last Sunday to join a group?

Pastor: 53.

Me: Out of the 53, how many were contacted by the small group leader?

Pastor [after looking up the number]**:** 27. [The number was effectively cut in half.]

Me: How many of those prospective members made it to a group?

Pastor: We don't know. [This is one of the largest churches in the country!]

While task-oriented means of filling groups appear to be efficient, they are not effective. By signing up online or filling out a card to be placed in a group by the church staff, the prospective group members are essentially being set up on a blind date. They don't know who the leader is. They don't know what house they're going to. They don't know if they will like anybody there, or if anyone will like them. More often than not, after the church staff moves heaven and earth to place someone in a group or sets up an online mechanism for connecting people into groups, many people were never contacted by the leader, so they don't attend the group or they attend for a relatively short time.

One day in the church office, our church's administrator said he had the solution for singles in the church. He proposed that we line up all of the single women on one side of the room and then line up all of the single men on the opposite side of the room. Then, not unlike a junior high dance, everyone would pick someone. After this revelation, the staff referred to him as "Mr. Romance." But isn't this what churches are doing to people who are looking for small groups? They place someone in a group and hope it works out!

The key to strong connections in small groups is relationship. As I said in the first sentence of *Exponential Groups*, "Everyone is already in a group." They have family, friends, coworkers, neighbors, acquaintances, fellow church members, and even other fans of their favorite sports teams. The key to forming lasting groups is to leverage the existing connections in a person's life to fill groups.

Lego Brick Exercise

In *Exponential Groups*, I share an analogy inspired by some thoughts from Leigh Anderson about how people are like Legos. The idea is that most people have a defined capacity for relationships just like a Lego brick has a defined number of dots to connect to other Legos (*EG* 127). Look at the drawing of a Lego below. If each dot represented the top eight relationships in your life, who would be on your Lego? Some people's Legos might look like this:

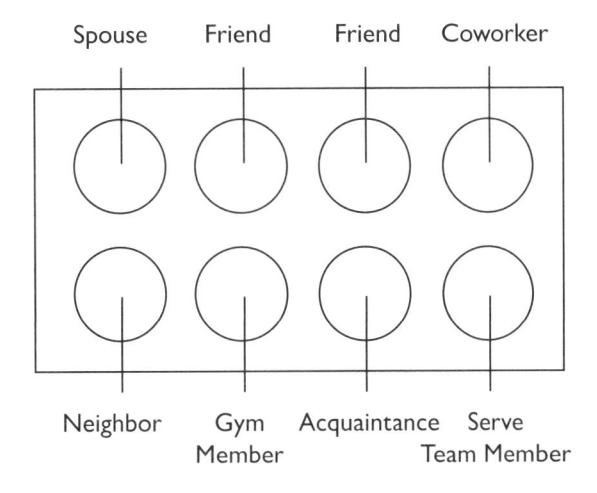

```
       Spouse    Friend    Friend    Coworker
          |        |         |          |
        ( O )    ( O )     ( O )      ( O )

        ( O )    ( O )     ( O )      ( O )
          |        |         |          |
       Neighbor   Gym    Acquaintance  Serve
                Member                Team Member
```

If a person's relational capacity is filled, then where does a small group fit in? In order to spend time with a group, the person has to forsake other relationships to make room for small group members. What if they don't like the small group members? What if they'd rather spend time with their friends? By asking people to displace their close relationships for the sake of joining a group and forming relationships with people they don't know, they just might reject the idea of joining a group all together. They already have close friends. Why do they need a group? But what if the people on their Lego were their group? By gathering the people they already know, they have an excuse to spend more time with those who are already in their lives and then be intentional about their spiritual growth. The church only needs to ask its members to list the people who are already in their lives and do a study with them or form a small group with them. Groups of friends tend to last longer than groups of strangers.

David Larson, our pastor at New Life, stood up one Sunday morning and asked our congregation to turn on their cell phones. I thought he'd lost his mind. This was back in 2004 before the advent of smartphones. Phones were only good for phone calls and texts. He asked our church to look at their speed dial list, and then he challenged everyone to invite the folks from this list to join them for a six-week study. After that, he asked everyone to turn their phones off and put them away.

For the average church member, we should encourage them to think about those people who are already in their life who would enjoy or benefit from a felt-needs study. Let's say the church was doing a series on relationships, marriage, family, hope, stress, living a balanced life, or something else. Who would they invite? Ask them to fill in their Legos or create some lists.

Relationship Lists Exercise

In the chart below, fill in the names of people who fit in each category in your life. You don't need to fill in every space. Who would enjoy or benefit from the study? Invite them!

Friends	Family	Neighbors	Coworkers	Church friends	Acquaintances

A list like this would make a great group! With a relevant topic, church members could gather with their friends or open their homes for their friends as well as others. This takes the hard work out of forming groups. By encouraging people to gather their friends to form a group, it also frees up small group pastors to invest in coaching and training their leaders. If the same effort most church staff put into recruiting leaders and placing people into groups was applied to coaching and training, then the church would get much farther faster in connecting people into groups and making disciples who make disciples.

Let Me Give You a 60-Second Seminar on Forming Lasting Groups

The best way to get into a group is to start the group yourself. If you're the leader, you're in!

The next best way to get into a group is by personal invitation. Group leaders invite people they know to join the group. If the groups have co-leaders, then they also invite people. Then, the people who are invited to the group also invite people they know. It's not important that everyone in the group knows the group leader, but it is significant that everyone in the group knows someone.

But what if someone is new to the church or to the community and truly doesn't know anyone?

The third wave of filling groups is by personal introduction. The group leaders and prospective members meet face-to-face, and then the prospective member decides which group to try for six weeks or so. While this may sound a little like the junior high dance, at least we've gone from blind dating to speed dating. In this way, the church creates an environment where leaders and prospective members could meet. This could be called a Connection Event or a Small Group Fair, and the format is basically an open house. Once the prospective members have had a chance to meet the leaders of open groups, then they choose a group to try. (More details for a Connection Event can be found later in this chapter.)

Passive Recruiting Methods	Active Recruiting Methods
Sign-Up Cards	Personal Invitation
Church Websites	Personal Introduction
Small Group Directories	Start a Group
Placement in a Group	"Do the Study with Your Friends"

The Connection Event or Small Group Fair

From the options in the "60-second seminar" above, the third best way of forming lasting groups is personal introduction. The Connection Event is the primary replacement for sign-up cards, church websites, and other passive recruiting methods. Again, people are moving from "blind dating" to "speed dating."

The Connection Event is simply an environment where prospective group members can meet group leaders face-to-face and sign up for a specific group. Think of a small group open house. Please note that the Connection Event is not a replacement for a personal invitation. Every group leader should personally invite people they know and ask God who should be invited to the group. In addition to personal invitation, the Connection Event can help to fill the group and offer an opportunity for those who weren't invited to join a group.

Connection Events can be used in two different ways: (1) to lead up to an alignment series or (2) to promote groups in general. If the Connection Event is used to form groups for an alignment series, then only the groups doing the alignment series should be featured at the event. This will avoid confusion for prospective members who are looking for a group doing the alignment study. If all of the church's various groups are featured, then the process of connecting with a group for the series becomes more complicated. This could even create an obstacle to someone joining a group. Keep the vision focused by only offering groups that are doing the series the senior pastor is promoting.

Connection Events can also be used to promote groups in general when there is not an alignment series or a church-wide campaign. Most churches will discover that after one to three years of forming groups with a sequence of church-wide campaigns, the campaign will begin to lose its effect (see chapter 12 for more on this). These churches will typically back off and launch maybe one alignment series per year. This is a great way to recruit new leaders and connect newcomers into groups. Groups, however, should be offered more than once per year.

Without reverting back to passive methods of recruiting, a Connection Event featuring all of a church's groups could be offered to promote groups when an alignment is not being used. My predecessor at Brookwood Church, David Hardy, established an annual "Small Group Sampler." All of the open groups and new groups in the church were represented at the event, regardless of what the group was studying. Each of the groups brought appetizers to share with prospective members, who would then circulate the room and "sample" the groups. During the course of the event, prospective members would sign up for the group they wanted to join.

> ## Case Study
> ## Christ Church
>
> Christ Church is a United Methodist Church in Fairview Heights, Illinois. They have been ranked as the third fastest UM church in the United States. "We have a transient church," said Pam Huff, former director of Connection and Discipleship (now retired). "Our town is around a military community, so we get a lot of visitors. We have experienced some rapid growth over the years."
>
> When she first came to the church, Pam found that the groups were pretty disorganized. "There was no organization whatsoever. Small groups were pretty new in the beginning. There had been a lack of leadership. If I did anything else, I put some organization into the small group ministry." Not only that, but she learned to leverage relationships in both forming groups and partnering new leaders with coaches.
>
> To connect people, the church started using church-wide campaigns, but they found that only a limited number of groups would continue. "At this point, we started to introduce the whole coaching system. I didn't have good luck getting them established with my old groups, but our new groups responded well." Pam looked over all of the church's experienced leaders and invited those she believed would be the most supportive of the small group ministry. "The new leaders would come to a training event and meet the coaches there. Originally, I would assign new leaders to coaches, but then the leaders didn't know who was calling them or why, even though I had told them they would get a call." By providing an opportunity for coaches to connect directly with the new leaders, natural connections formed, and the coaching relationship began.
>
> For group formation, the church didn't put a lot of requirements on new leaders except for inviting members to their groups. "My only real requirement was that someone was a Christian. I would usually have a face-to-face contact with them, but there was no real vetting process for new leaders. We really encouraged people to do a lot of inviting themselves."
>
> The church supplemented personal invitations with opportunities for the congregation to sign up for specific groups after the worship service. "We would introduce the leaders during the service so people could put a face with a name. Then the leaders would stand by their sign-up sheets in our Scripture Hall, which was a big gathering area." People would sign up for the specific group they wanted to join.
>
> The church found that personal invitation and personal introduction at these sign-up events were far superior to assigning people to groups. "Sometimes people would fill out a card in the service indicating they wanted to join a group. When I reached out to them, I would never hear back from them. It's almost like they were surprised that somebody actually contacted them." By providing more active methods of forming groups, such as invitations and in-person sign-up opportunities, more people found their way into groups without all of the work of processing sign-up cards that never really netted many results.

How to Host a Connection Event or Small Group Fair

A Connection Event can occur immediately following a worship service or as a stand-alone event on an afternoon or evening. Connection Events hosted after worship services tend to have higher sign-up rates but lower show-up rates. There is a bit of a captive audience as people are exiting the service, yet signing up for a group can be more of an impulsive or emotional decision that some do not follow through with. The key to filling groups this way is for group leaders to allow more people to sign up than the number the leader ideally wants in the group, knowing that not everyone will show up for the group. While an effort should be made to contact and include everyone who signs up, the reality is that not everyone will. That's okay.

If the Connection Event is hosted as a stand-alone event apart from a worship service, far fewer people will attend the event; however, the commitment rate is much higher. These prospective group members made an effort to attend an event specifically for the purpose of signing up for a group. They will follow through for the most part.

The location of the Connection Event is significant, especially if it follows a worship service, and should take place on the way out of the sanctuary or auditorium. If the event is in a more remote location, then people will be more likely to pick up their children from their classes or head to the parking lot. The event should be held somewhere in the flow as people are leaving. On one occasion, we held a Connection Event in the church auditorium around the perimeter. People left their seats and went directly to the group type or location noted on a sign by the group leaders.

On this is an example of a flyer to promote a Connection Event submitted by Elliot Diaz, Small Group Pastor at Manna Church in Fayetteville, North Carolina.

The reverse side of the flyer could include a list of available groups arranged either by location or day of the week. For larger churches, this might seem logistically impossible, because the list could potentially contain hundreds or even thousands of groups. If the group leaders have been inviting people to join their groups prior to the Connection Event, then the task of connecting people into available groups should be less daunting, since many people will have already joined a group or many groups are already full.

If the flyer is distributed to the congregation during the worship service, then prospective group members could review the list of available groups and circle those they are interested in. Then they know exactly who to talk to at the Connection Event.

Arranging the Room for a Connection Event or Small Group Fair

Different types of groups should be arranged so prospective members can easily find the group they are looking for, and so signage is crucial at the event. It's important also to remember that the room will look different with a large group of people than it does when it's empty. Signs should be clear and placed up high enough so they can easily be seen.

If the Connection Event is large, then a map showing the placement of different types of groups should be available. Prospective members will know exactly where they need to go to sign up for a specific type of group. Also, small group leaders who are not participating in the event and coaches should be available to serve as greeters during the event to personally direct prospective group members.

Small Group Solutions

No matter how well a church has listed, labeled, and arranged their small group leaders, there will always be some who need a little help to find a group. It's a good idea to have some greeters—small group coaches, leaders of closed groups, or other helpful folks—who are on the lookout for anyone who seems confused. If the greeter can help them, then the problem is solved.

To provide answers, it would be helpful to have a Small Group Solutions table equipped with computers logged into the small group database, a map showing every group's geographic location, and staff who know about specific groups. This way, when some can't locate group from a list, they can look at a map and find a group right by their houses. Once a group is located, then a staff member or greeter should walk the prospective group member over to the group's leader and introduce them.

Sometimes the solution for those who can't locate a group that meets on the day or near the location they need is to suggest they start their own group with people they know. Many groups have been started on the spot in this exact scenario.

(Figure I) Small Group Fair, Manna Church, Fayetteville, NC

Connection Event Checklist

- [ ] Tables and tablecloths for each group
- [ ] Signs for each group
- [ ] Directional signs for group types: Men, Women, Couples, Singles, Zip Codes/Towns, etc.
- [ ] A Small Group Directory listing all of the groups by type and/or day
- [ ] Recruit Connection Event greeters to offer direction to different groups
- [ ] Sign-up sheets
- [ ] Pens
- [ ] Clipboards
- [ ] Two or more computers
- [ ] A large monitor to display group locations
- [ ] Copies of the curriculum for groups that start on the spot

If the church is hosting a "Sampler" event, then the checklist should also include plates, napkins, utensils, cups, ice, and drinks.

Below is a map of a Connection Event at Olive Branch Community Church in Corona, California, along with a picture of the actual event:

(Figure 2) Used with permission of Justin Ristow, Olive Branch Community Church

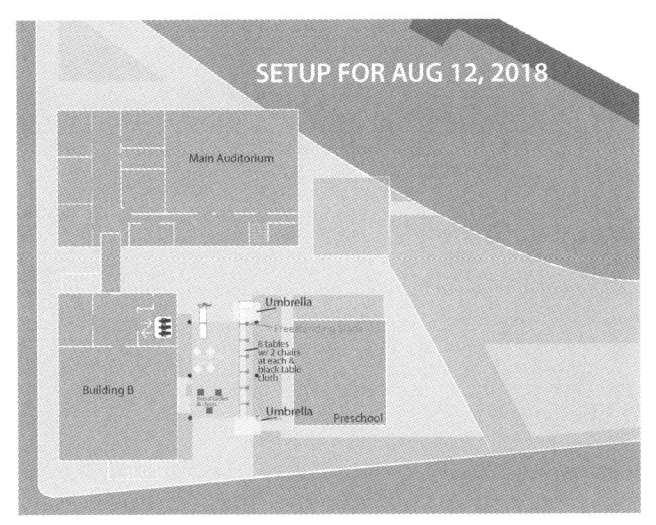

(Figure 3) Used with permission of Justin Ristow, Olive Branch Community Church

Each group should produce an information sheet for their group with the leader's name, location, day and time, directions, childcare instructions, and any other information a new group member will need for the first meeting. Here is an example:

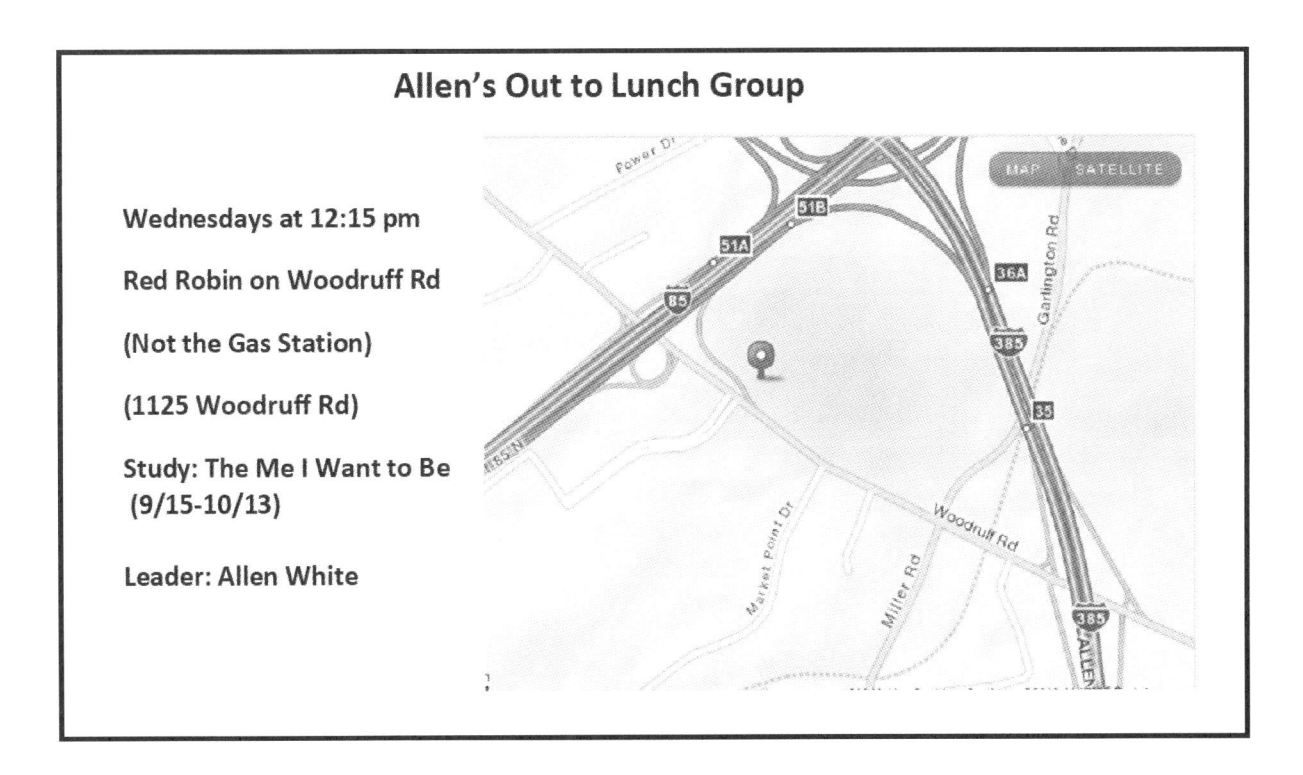

Allen's Out to Lunch Group

Wednesdays at 12:15 pm

Red Robin on Woodruff Rd

(Not the Gas Station)

(1125 Woodruff Rd)

Study: The Me I Want to Be (9/15-10/13)

Leader: Allen White

Small Group Connection Instructions for Group Leaders

1. Find table with your affinity (men, women, couples, singles, parents) or location

    North of the church: Mauldin, Greenville, Taylors, Greer, Duncan

    South of the church: Simpsonville (Downtown, Georgia Road, Fairview); Fountain Inn; Hickory Tavern; Laurens

    East of the church: Five Forks/Scuffletown/Hwy. 14

    West of the church: Easley/Powdersville; groups at the church

2. Meet your prospective members

3. Sign up new members for your specific group

    No "interest" lists

    Don't lose control of your list (you might get forty people!)

    Sign up about 50 percent more than you can handle (10 new = 15 sign-ups)

4. Trouble finding a group? Small Group Solutions: located at the North/South Featured Ministry Tables

    Longer than three-minute conversation? Send them to Small Group Solutions.

    Meet the other hosts who will be near you. Your group might not be the right fit, but someone standing near you might have the right group.

Sample Letter to Small Group Leaders about the Connection Event

Dear Small Group Hosts and Leaders,

We are so glad that you are leading a group for "The Story" that starts on Sunday, March 29. We believe that this will be a powerful series your group will truly enjoy.

The **Small Group Connection** is this Sunday, March 22, after each service in the concourse. We would like each group studying "The Story" to be represented after every service this Sunday (and next Sunday, March 29). The task is simple: meet prospective group members and sign them up for the five-week study. Find the banner for your group for either the location (north, south, east, or west of the church) or affinity (Men, Women, Parents, Couples, or Singles).

Please meet us at 9:20 a.m. on Sunday in the concourse for last-minute instructions.

Also, for those of you who want to **preorder books** through the bookstore this week, we are doing this a little differently from before. If you have collected money from your group ($10 per book) or you are paying for the books yourself, feel free to order books anytime this week from the bookstore. Then, you or one representative from your group should pick up the books on Sunday and distribute them at your next meeting. Individual members can purchase a copy of the book on their own this Sunday. The bookstore is not reserving books that are not paid for in advance. Thanks for your understanding in this. It's quite an undertaking to distribute three thousand books in two weeks.

I'm looking forward to seeing you on Sunday!

God bless,

Allen White
Adult Discipleship Pastor

Connection Event Group Sign-Up Sheet

Group Name: _____

Group Location: _____

Meeting Day and Time: _____

Name	E-mail	Phone	Number of Children

The Structure

Chapter 8

Sustaining Groups

Groups don't last after alignment series or church-wide campaigns for primarily two reasons: either they weren't invited to continue, or they didn't start in the first place. Churches have lamented the fall off from church-wide campaigns or have avoided alignment series all together because of this. Yet, both of these issues can be prevented.

At the risk of being obvious, groups that don't start tend to not continue (*EG* 81)! The encouragement of a coach can help new group leaders overcome the discouragement leaders might face in forming their groups. New leaders are hit with a lot: rejection by prospective group members, the busyness of life, discouragement, distraction, and even outright spiritual warfare. A relationship with a coach can help the new leaders realize they are not the only ones facing these problems and that it wasn't a bad idea for them to start a group. The coach can help to reframe what new leaders face and encourage them to continue. Coaching works best when the new leader meets the coach at the New Leader Briefing and the coach begins weekly phone calls in the week following the Briefing. (See chapter 4 for more.)

In many alignment series, the initial invitation to the congregation is to lead for a short-term study of six weeks or so. Reflecting on the thoughts from chapter 8 of *Exponential Groups* and the research of Everett Rogers found in his book *Diffusion of Innovations*, the alignment series is a short-term trial run at leading a group. In Rogers's research, this is step three of five in the process of adapting a new idea. In other words, deciding to lead a group for a six-week alignment series is not the finish line. It's the starting line. There is no guarantee these new leaders will continue leading their groups. By offering a concrete next step for these prospective leaders, you can improve the odds of the groups continuing.

In the middle of the trial run, a specific next step study should be offered to new leaders. Don't allow these new leaders to become lost in a sea of choices. Choose the study for them. They usually won't have much of an opinion anyway. Think about using a study on how to be a small group, such as *Community: Starting a Healthy Group* by yours truly. A series like this could be used for every new group the church starts. (This is not necessary for established groups. They can return to their regular pattern of meeting.) The only decision a new group should be asked to make is whether or not they will continue.

If the alignment series is six weeks, then the next-step study should be offered by at least week three or four, so the group will have two or three weeks to talk about continuing as a group. The group should decide before the last week of the study. If not, they may not continue once they disband.

Below is a flyer advertising a next-step study from Northwoods Community Church in Peoria, Illinois. Since this church has a longer established small group ministry, a primary next step is offered to all of the groups, especially new groups, and other options are given for more experienced groups.

Is your group finished with STORM shelter? *What's next?*

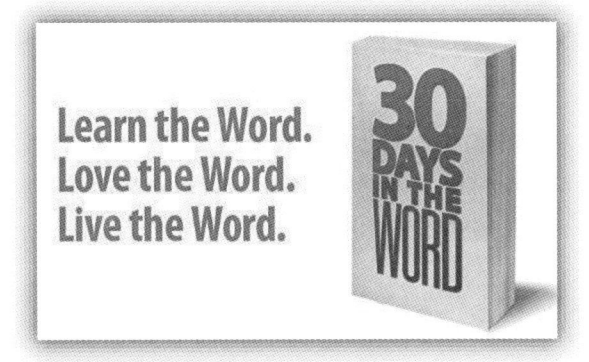

We highly recommend your group continues on this path of spiritual growth together with another great study by Pastor Cal...

30 Days in the Word – 5 week study
Through Bible reading, video lessons, group discussion, and practice, take a journey into God's Word. Learn how to get the most out of the Bible. Grow to love how the Word draws you closer to God. And come to live out the Word's ways and wisdom. Learn the Word. Love the Word. Live the Word.

Every week you'll have the opportunity to take more steps on your Bible journey. This 30 day adventure is especially designed to be done with a group of fellow journeyers, and we believe you'll get the most out of the experience in that context. We are providing the reading plan, video teaching, discussion guides, and practice exercise for everyone in your group to use.

OTHER *great group studies created by Pastor Cal and Northwoods Small Group Ministry...*

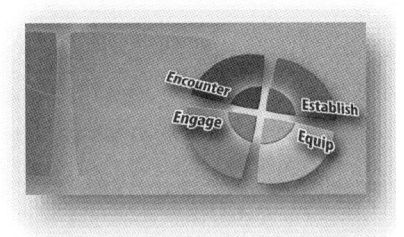

E4 - Empowered for Supernatural Living – 4 week study
"That you may be filled to the measure of all the fullness of Christ." That's a mind-blowing statement! God created each of us to be a catalyst for life-change, a super-natural agent of life transformation. Discover how to become empowered for supernatural living as your group experiences video teachings, discussion guide, a spiritual health assessment and group connection as you actively support each other.

Exponential – 5 week study
Two thousand years ago, Jesus walked up to a handful of people and said, *"Follow me!"* Now, through the Exponential study, you can explore what it means to be a disciple of Jesus Christ. Gather with your group and embark together on a five-week journey toward a life of increasing impact, true community and eternal purpose! Resources will be provided for you to help your group thrive such as video teachings, discussion guide and *"Multiply"* book by Francis Chan.

Home Run – 6 week study
Just like in the game of baseball, the way to win in life involves a clear path, some guiding principles, a great team, and a lot of fun. Through this study, you'll come to understand that advancing toward victory in life is like rounding the bases in baseball. You can't skip any bases if you want a home run. Join with a group of friends as you experience video teachings, a relevant study guide, and *"Home Run"* book by Kevin Meyers as you discover what it means to live a Home Run life!

(Used by permission of John Chaney, Northwoods Church, Peoria, Illinois.)

To help the leaders and groups with the decision-making process, it's important to offer them options in case the leader cannot continue leading the group. Think about the possible objections. Maybe the leader didn't count on more than a six-week commitment and can't continue. Would another member of the group be interested in leading the group? Maybe the leader is hosting all of the meetings in their home and it's too much for them to do. Could another group member open their home for the group? Maybe the group leader is doing the majority of the work. Could other group members share the load? Maybe the leader hasn't considered the group continuing. Ask them!

There are three things a small group pastor can use to introduce the next step and help group leaders make a decision about leading: a survey, a mid-series meeting, and their coaches. Each of these will work in conjunction with the others to gauge the group leaders' interest or objections and help them to overcome their objections. Please note: If a group leader simply cannot continue leading the group, then be gracious to them. I've seen group leaders stop leading after a six-week series only to return a year later and start a group that continues.

The mid-series survey is a way to take the temperature of group leaders and have a "meeting before the meeting." The survey will give some indication of what the group leaders intend or what they are struggling with. This information will help the small group pastor and coaches know what they're walking into at the mid-series meeting, and it will help the coach know how to guide the group leaders in making their decisions about continuing.

The best vehicle to deliver the mid-series survey is an online survey tool, which will tabulate the results as well as allow individual responses to be viewed. If this is not available or appears to be too complicated, then the questions could be sent via e-mail to the leaders. The last resort might be a paper version of the survey.

Sample Mid-Series Survey

Thank you for stepping out to start a new group for the series. We hope that you are enjoying the series and are growing as a group. Please take a few minutes to give us a little feedback on your experience so far.

1. Your Information
   - Name:
   - Co-Leader's Name:
   - Group Name:
   - Cell Phone Number:
   - E-mail Address:

2. Who is your coach?

3. How many times has your coach contacted you since you signed up to start your group?
   - ☐ Never
   - ☐ 1–2 times
   - ☐ 3–5 times
   - ☐ 6 or more times

4. How has your coach helped you the most in the course of this study?

5. What have you enjoyed the most about leading your group?

6. What issues or concerns have surfaced in your group? (this is completely confidential)

7. In the study so far, has your group . . . (check ALL that apply)
- ☐ Rotated leadership by having different members lead the discussion?
- ☐ Met in different members' homes?
- ☐ Had different members provide refreshments?
- ☐ Used the video teaching?
- ☐ Used the Group Agreement and Guidelines?
- ☐ Completed most of the study each week?
- ☐ Kept up with the pastor's weekly messages? (This is Week 3)

8. How is God working in your group? (open-ended question)

9. Do you plan to continue leading your group after this study is over?
- ☐ Yes
- ☐ No
- ☐ Still deciding

10. If you do not plan to continue leading your group, what has your group considered? (check ALL that apply) *[Use Skip Logic in the survey tool, so this question is offered only to those who responded "No" or "Still Deciding" in the previous question.]*
- ☐ Fulfilling your six-week commitment to the study
- ☐ Asking another group member to lead the group
- ☐ Asking other group members to host the group in their homes
- ☐ Participating in a future study, but not right now
- ☐ Joining with another group
- ☐ Our group never really started

11. The church is offering a new study called *Community: Starting a Healthy Group* by Allen White as a next step for your group. What are your group's intentions for your next study? (check ALL that apply)
- ☐ Doing the *Community* study
- ☐ Reviewing the *Community* study
- ☐ Considering a different study
- ☐ Other, please specify:

12. What is one burning question you have about your group?

When responses are received, the information should be communicated with the coach. Coaches should reach out to any of the groups that have stated they won't continue or that are undecided. While the coach should not pressure leaders to continue if they are unable or unwilling, the coach should investigate their objections and offer possible alternatives so the group might continue. Often group leaders assume that if they cannot continue to lead the group, then the group can no longer meet. If given the opportunity, group members may want to continue with the leader as a member of the group or continue without the leader.

Mid-Series Meeting

The purpose of the mid-series meeting is to receive feedback on the series and the groups, as well as to secure the commitment of group leaders to continue. Combined with the survey, this meeting can help to identify any issues with the series or in the groups. Issues can range from problems with the curriculum materials to unclear instructions given in the study to group dynamics. If it's possible, group leaders should sit with their coaches during the meeting. Meetings like this will typically attract 50 percent or fewer of the group leaders; but between the meeting, the survey, and the coach contacts, feedback can be given by practically every group leader. The agenda for the mid-series meeting is relatively simple:

1. What's working?

   Affirm the responses given by the group leaders. Ask clarifying questions if appropriate.

2. What's not working?

   Ask the leaders to explain. Ask the room if others are facing the same issue. Ask if any other leaders have found a solution. Refer particular issues to coaches.

3. What's next?

   This question should be used to talk about the next-step study, show a sample of the teaching video and study guide, and answer questions. The responses of specific groups about continuing should be addressed at the tables between the coaches and leaders. If the leaders have completed the series and/or have talked to the coach previously about their groups' intentions about continuing, then there should not be too many surprises in this meeting.

The mid-series meeting will offer insights into several different areas. First, the meeting will reveal any current struggles the group leaders are facing. If the same issues are shared by multiple groups, then the issues will merit a response from the small group pastor either by e-mail or via video, so the leaders not in attendance can benefit. More than likely, it won't be possible to pull all of the leaders back together for another meeting anytime soon.

Second, the mid-series meeting will give a glimpse into the relationships between leaders and their coaches. How well do the coaches and leaders seem to know one another? Their engagement around the tables will reveal how familiar they are with one another. If the coaches have been in regular contact with their leaders, then they will appear to know one another. If the contacts have not been made, then the conversations will probably be more basic or even stilted. Although this is not the final test of whether coaches are doing well, it is an indication.

Lastly, this meeting should solidify the commitment of group leaders to continue their groups into the next series. If the groups haven't completely decided, then the coaches should continue to connect with the group leaders, help them overcome objections to continuing, and report back on the groups' decisions to continue or discontinue meeting.

If groups are formed with the more active and more relational methods of personal invitation and personal introduction mentioned in chapter 7, then they have a much better chance of lasting. In addition, the involvement of a coach to encourage and support group leaders is a powerful way to help groups start as well as continue. By introducing a concrete next step for the group, most groups should continue. I've seen 80 percent or more of the groups in an alignment series continue by following this pattern.

Chapter 9

Leadership Track

Once a group has completed two consecutive studies or alignment series, they are pretty much set to continue as a group. Referring back to Everett Rogers's five steps in adopting a new idea, the group has passed from the trial run (step 3) to implementation (step 4). In the implementation stage, a person chooses to put the new idea to use. They had a good experience in the trial run and want to move forward with the group. This is where the next step curriculum comes in (*EG* 157). The final step in this process is confirmation in which the group and its leader decide to continue as a group. Once the group and its leader have indicated their intent to continue, either by making an overt commitment or by simply continuing to meet together, it's time to assess their developing needs and offer additional resources as the leaders need them.

Now, a word of caution: How things are navigated from this point forward will greatly determine whether these new groups thrive or disappear. There are some small group pastors (I won't mention any names at risk of implicating myself!) who at this point will have tolerated all of this lowering the bar and letting anybody lead stuff for long enough. They feel that now it's time to get back to business. If they put off requirements for the test drive, then it's time to bring them back! This is partially correct.

Once group leaders have reached this point, they need more than they've been offered up thus far. On the other side, now that leaders have had the experience of leading their group through a couple of studies, they probably have more questions about leading groups than before. But here is the tricky part: Not all of the leaders are at exactly the same place in their leadership. They don't all need the same things at the same rate in the same way as other leaders. This is where the requirements that the church delayed need to return and where great patience must be exercised.

I've actually witnessed small group pastors breath a sign of relief after an alignment series ends, and they attempt to raise the bar immediately. The problem with such an abrupt change from "get together with your friends and do the study" to now "you must be official to lead" is that some leaders and groups will get lost in the transition. Groups that were comfortable in starting a group on their terms (*EG* 135–43) won't be prepared to immediately embrace these new terms. The consequence of suddenly mandating requirements is that some groups will locate more video-based curriculum, continue meeting, and go underground. The big issue here is that the church can no longer communicate with groups that aren't interacting with their coaches and that are no longer on the church's radar.

The hope is that the group leaders who have chosen to continue will embrace the church's requirements for group leaders. But, at this point, the requirements are probably more important to the church's leaders than to the groups' leaders. This is where patience comes in.

Going back to the list of requirements your church chose to delay in chapter 3 of this workbook, your church has legitimate reasons for asking small group leaders to complete these items—church membership, a growth track, small group basic training, and whatever else you normally require. It's good for the church to qualify its leaders. And it's good for the leaders to be well equipped for the role they serve.

Exercise: Bringing Back the Requirements

Requirement	Reason for Requirement	Expected Timeline	How to Invite

In this exercise, it's important to articulate the reasons for the requirements so leaders will understand why these requirements are necessary to both the church and to them as a leader. This is a good exercise for church leadership, since churches can sometimes require things but not completely understand the purpose themselves. For instance, while many churches have church membership, they're not always sure why it's important. If the church doesn't know why church membership is important, then how can they expect anyone else to know? But if the church sees church membership as a way of communicating what the church believes, what the church values, and how the church works, then they can communicate the importance of these things to prospective church members (and group leaders). Becoming a member signifies agreement with what the church considers to be important. Do this exercise for all of the requirements you delayed, and don't be surprised if some of the requirements no longer seem as important as they did earlier.

Once you understand the reason behind your requirements and how they will benefit new group leaders, invite the leaders to attend the membership class (maybe with their whole group), small group basic training, growth track, and whatever else the church wants their leaders to participate in. Invitation and patience will go a long way toward securing leaders' cooperation, and most new leaders will follow the church's lead. It's usually good to offer multiple opportunities to fulfill the requirements. Leaders might be open and willing to meet these requirements but have schedule conflicts that prevent them from doing so.

Most new leaders should complete the church's requirements in six months to one year. If there are leaders who have not started down this leadership track after a year or more of leading a group, then a personal conversation is probably in order to find out what's going on. It could be as simple as a schedule conflict or just a lack of follow-through. In a few cases, there might be resistance to the church's leadership. This is a more serious issue, and the person closest to the leader should sit down with them. If the leader has a coach, then the conversation should start with the pastor. If the leader resists the coach's inquiry, then the small group pastor might need to become involved. Use the Leadership Pathway Chart to track each leader's progress.

Small Group Basic Training

As discussed in *Exponential Groups* (178–200), here is a basic outline of what could be included in Basic Training. Some of these things will not be new to your group leaders, but this will be an opportunity to explain the reasons behind what they are doing and how groups are done at the church.

Training Outline

- The Biblical Basis for Groups
- The Importance of a Group Agreement
- The Relationship with a Coach
- Sharing Ownership in the Group
- Balancing Group Time between Developing Relationships and Completing Lessons
- Encouraging Group Members to Share Openly
- Avoiding Rabbit Trails in Group Discussions
- What If You Don't Know All of the Answers?
- Choosing Curriculum for Your Group
- When to Refer a Group Member for Help
- Group Life Cycle: When Should My Group Break Up?
- Group Reports

The church may decide to include other items that are important to the groups and to the church. Do whatever best serves the leaders and the church. Typically, I've offered small group basic training in a two- to three-hour session. You may choose to do the same or offer increments of the training in shorter sessions.

Small Group Leader Job Description

As leaders move forward toward the "Step 5: Confirmation stage" in Everett Rogers's model for adopting new ideas, the requirements also increase. Here is a sample job description and expectations provided by Elliot Diaz, small group pastor at Manna Church in Fayetteville, North Carolina.

Expectation for Leaders (Section 3 of *A Guide to Getting Started*)

As a Manna Church Small Group Leader, I Will:

o Passionately live out Manna's three core values: Love God, Love Each Other, and Love the World.

o Understand and comply with the By-Laws of Manna Church.

o Support Manna's leadership, vision, and Small Group philosophy in what I say and do.

o Model a lifestyle of personal and spiritual growth.

o Be open to counsel from my Site's Small Group leadership and provide them with highlights and concerns about my group regularly. (This includes responding to all requests for information and surveys that you receive from Manna Church's Small Group leadership team.)

- Respond within two days to prospective Small Group members.
- Strive to achieve the three goals of Small Groups (Meet, Mentor, Multiply) and follow the other
- Traffic Laws provided by Manna's Small Group leadership team.

- **Meet (create a relational environment)**
  - Shoulder-tap potential members (starting with my sphere of influence or *oikos*) for my Small Group.
  - Pray for and coordinate weekly Small Group meetings to include fellowship, a topic or activity, and a spiritual component.
  - Pray regularly for everyone in my Small Group.
  - Identify and/or organize childcare needs.

- **Mentor (help people reach their next level of faith)**
  - Encourage and challenge people to experience real transformation in their lives on a consistent, habit-forming basis.
  - Help participants discover and develop their giftings.
  - Care for the needs of the people in my group to the best of my ability. (If a need is beyond your ability to help, reach out to your Site Pastor for assistance.)
  - Encourage my group members to attend the Growth Track.

- **Multiply**
  - Disciples: Conduct at least one outreach throughout the cycle (either group-initiated or with the church).
  - Identify an assistant leader for my group.
  - Intentionally raise up new leaders (encourage my group members to attend Leader Step).

Manna also provides specific definitions of a small group for their congregation as groups from an alignment series move toward becoming on-going groups in the church.

Small Group Traffic Laws

GREEN (Required)

1. Meet (Fellowship)
The Small Group should be a place where members can connect and form friendships.

2. Mentor (Growing balanced disciples)
God is always calling his children to grow. The Small Group Leader helps members reach their next level as they discover, develop, and deploy their gifts. Share ownership. You may be perfectly capable of opening up your home, bringing the food, and leading the discussion each time you meet, but when you allow others to help, you give them an opportunity to grow. Think through how you will delegate responsibilities in your group. Consider asking someone to co-lead or to assist you in leading, asking people to organize food for the meeting, selecting people to coordinate outreaches for the group, etc.

3. Multiply

Disciples: The Small Group should spur on the members to do their part in helping the lost come to know Jesus. Each cycle, plan at least one outreach.

Leaders: In every Small Group, there is at least one person whose next step is leading a group of their own. The Small Group Leader should identify them, encourage them, and empower them to lead. Encourage Leader Step.

Groups: If applicable, reproduce your group.

YELLOW (Open to interpretation and/or requiring caution)

1. Use discretion when handling sensitive or controversial subjects.

2. Controversial or sensitive issues can quickly become sticky. If you are planning to teach on or discuss a subject like this, talk to your leadership beforehand. If someone in your group brings up something difficult, listen to the Holy Spirit and end the discussion when it's appropriate.

3. Operate within the yearly Small Group cycles.

4. There are three Small Group cycles per year: winter/spring, summer, and fall. These cycles are designed to be an easy on/off ramp, allowing participants and leaders to continue their groups, attend new ones, or take a break if needed. Use cycle breaks to recharge and rest prior to the next cycle.

5. Frequency.

6. Regular meetings build trust within the group and increase its effectiveness. All Small Groups are encouraged to meet weekly, bimonthly at the very least.

7. Be open to accepting anyone into your Small Group.

8. Create an atmosphere that is inviting to anyone interested in your group.

9. Welcome diverse opinions.

10. Differences of opinion between the leader and group members are acceptable, as long they don't cause confusion or disruption. If the dynamic is going in a negative direction, the leader will need to address the situation appropriately.

RED (Not permitted)

1. No two-member Small Groups.
A Small Group should always be three people or more. A two-person Small Group constitutes one of three things: a friendship, a date, or trouble. NO alone time with a member of the opposite sex who is not your spouse.

2. No domination of the group dynamic.
A Small Group leader is there to facilitate ministry, not dominate it. A good ratio for conversation is 30 percent Small Group Leader, 70 percent the rest of the group.

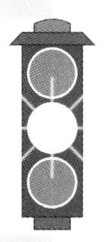

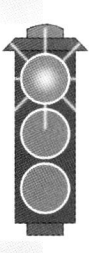

3. Do not teach contrary to the beliefs of Manna Church.

Manna Church's theological stances are basic evangelical Christian beliefs, including baptism of the Holy Spirit and the charismatic gifts. These are outlined in the church's by-laws, available upon request. Small Group Leaders may hold different theological beliefs; HOWEVER, they are not permitted to teach those beliefs in their Small Groups.

4. Don't try to handle every difficult situation.

Some issues that come up in the group will be within your ability to handle. But when a serious issue arises and you feel overwhelmed, refer to your leadership.

How to get benched as a Small Group Leader

1. **Rebellion**: Stay faithful, humble, and teachable.

2. **Concerns about your relationships,** especially your marriage (if applicable).

3. **Bad fruit**: Attitudes are contagious—you will reproduce who you are.

These symptoms typically result from a lack of intimacy with God, which is the most important qualification for a leader.

The thing to remember in the leadership track is that this is the culmination of a recruiting process that started with an alignment series, then continued into a next step study, and then developed into an on-going group. What at one time was an answer to the question "Do you want to lead a group?" is now a process that takes six to twelve months rather than a simple yes or no answer. (Remember, I was receiving mostly no's before I changed approaches!)

Chapter 10

Coaching and Training

When a small group pastor complained to me that his leaders didn't attend his training meetings, I told him, "Well, your leaders don't show up because your training is boring and irrelevant."

He was a little insulted and became defensive. "How do you know my training is boring and irrelevant? You've never been to my meetings."

"Well, that's why my leaders stopped coming to my meetings."

The problem with generic training meetings is that group leaders and their circumstances are not generic. No two leaders are exactly alike. Granted, when leaders first start, they need more help. They've never led a group before. They don't know how to run a meeting. They need some direction and instruction to pull this off. But once leaders gain some experience, they no longer need as much direction. Experienced leaders need trouble-shooting when their groups face problems. They need to set goals for themselves and their groups. They need support, encouragement, and accountability, but they won't necessarily get this from sitting in rows at a meeting.

The problem with most small group leader training is that it appeals to the least common denominator—the new leader. The training can't leave the new leader behind, but the training also can't take experienced leaders back to kindergarten. Training works when what the leader needs is delivered when the leader needs it. Effective training can come from a coach, a video, a blog post, or a book. Considering most group leaders' limited time and availability, most people are not available for frequent meetings or training events. So how do you train them?

Limit Large Meetings, Multiply Small Meetings

I chose to limit the training events in the churches I served to just two events per year: a Fall Sneak Peek meeting to rally experienced leaders for an alignment series and to take a trial run at coaching (see chapter 4 of this workbook for the Sneak Peek agenda) and an annual small group leaders' retreat. These are both large-scale vision casting events that set the tone for the year and keep the purpose and goals for groups in front of the leaders. More specific training should be delivered in more specific coaching and training.

After years of inflicting the training I thought leaders needed on them in monthly meetings, I found I was often answering questions no one was asking—or worse yet, I sometimes had to invent agendas for the sake of having a meeting! If there is no reason for a meeting, then there shouldn't be a meeting. Talk about boring and irrelevant.

The best way to know what training leaders need is to ask them. That might be the simplest yet most profound discovery I've made in training leaders. What are they struggling with? What issues are coming up in their groups? What obstacles do they need to overcome? But how do you get this information?

Survey Your Leaders

Surveys are great tools to get specific data from group leaders. They can be used to update group rosters (see chapter 11), to get feedback on curriculum, to determine the next steps for leaders and groups (see chapter 8), and to take the temperature of leaders. By asking leaders what problems their group is facing or what issues are surfacing in their groups, the small group pastor instantly has a list of the specific training needs of group leaders.

I also discovered that leaders would write things on a survey they would never dream of saying to my face. If I asked leaders in person for feedback on a curriculum I had written, they would just as soon "Bless my heart" rather than give specific feedback. On a survey, however, they would be open and honest about what they thought—even though they knew the survey was from me. To get a list of specific issues group leaders are facing, ask questions such as:

- What's working in your group?
- What's not working in your group?
- What specific problems or issues is your group facing?

These questions probably seem like a no-brainer, but if you don't ask specific questions, you don't get specific answers. More examples of surveys are given in chapters 8 and 11 of this workbook.

Talk to Your Coaches and Small Group Team

Coaches are the first line of information on what leaders are dealing with. Whether the information comes from conversations with your coaches and small group team or from monthly reports (see chapter 11), the goal is not to explore every specific issue group leaders are facing, but to spot the trends that are occurring across the small group ministry as a whole. As you'll see later in this chapter, coaches are the best training tools available to small group leaders. That being said, the small group pastor is responsible for the ministry as a whole. You can't give that away. While coaches should be empowered to train and help their leaders, they also need to report to the small group team and/or small group pastor.

Talk to Your Leaders

Without getting in the way of coaches, it's also important for small group pastors to connect directly with small group leaders. This is not to interfere with the coaching structure, but to keep a pulse on the small group ministry as a whole.

My friend, Alan Pace in Nashville, came up with the idea of meeting with groups of small group leaders on a monthly basis in an informal setting. These meetings are set for one week out of each month for breakfast, coffee, or lunch to hear from leaders about their groups. I limited the attendance at these meetings to five leaders per meeting, and they could join only one of these meetings per year. (At Brookwood Church, we had over four hundred leaders, and I got the feeling a few of them might have let me buy their lunch every month!)

Every month, an e-mail invitation was sent out to the group leaders, and then they responded to schedule which meeting they chose to attend that month. Once the limit of five leaders was reached for each meeting, then the meeting was closed. The leaders could choose another meeting that week, or they could wait until the following month.

The meeting format was simple. The leaders went around the table to introduce themselves to the group, and then the discussion turned to what's working/not working. There were discussions of specific issues. There were also many conversations about curriculum recommendations. More often than not, the leaders would answer each other's questions. In fact, most of the time I felt like a fly on the wall, making notes about what the groups were dealing with. At times, it seemed that my most valuable contribution was arranging the meeting and picking up the check (which I included as part of the budget).

At first, there was a little misunderstanding with my coaches. They sensed that I was interfering or taking over. After all, why did they need to coach if I was going to meet with the leaders? Truthfully, I didn't have a good answer until I heard Jack Welch, former CEO of General Electric, speak at a conference.[13] As CEO, he would visit GE's factories and talk to the workers on the assembly line. Welch admitted that this threatened his vice presidents, but his reasoning was that if he didn't get in there and talk to the workers, then he wouldn't know what was going on in his company. That was all the justification I needed.

How to Address Common Issues without Meetings

Issues affecting multiple groups can be addressed more broadly to all of the group leaders. I took the list of issues my leaders gave me from surveys and conversations, and I wrote weekly blog posts to address each issue. My blog at allenwhite.org actually started from answering questions from my leaders. All of the leaders were subscribed to a distribution list and received a weekly post with an answer to one of the questions they were asking. Today, I encourage churches to create two-minute videos they can push out to their leaders with solutions to these larger issues. It's also a good idea to have a place to archive these answers in case what is addressed this week may not be their issue until six months from now.

Another approach is to distribute resources to every coach and small group leader. One year, I purchased two cases of *Making Small Groups Work* by Henry Cloud and John Townsend (Zondervan, 2003) and gave a copy to every one of our group leaders and coaches. Other resources that can be used as training resources or even leader appreciation gifts could include:

- *The Nine Keys to Effective Small Group Leadership* by Carl George and Warren Bird (CDLM, 2007)
- *Leading Healthy Groups* by Allen White (AWC, 2018)
- *Leading Small Groups with Purpose* by Steve Gladen (Baker Books, 2011)

The final method of delivering training and casting vision to group leaders is an annual small group leaders' retreat. While this is a meeting per se, there is something to be said for taking leaders off-campus and creating a special occasion for focused training. In many cases, the leaders could quote specific things they learned on the retreat six months after we returned. The training stuck!

Here is an example of a weekly training e-mail to all of the leaders that includes a link to video training provided by Kevin Yoder, Campus Pastor of Rivertown Community Church in Marianna, Florida.

Stay Connected: Group Essential #1

There are eight Leader Essentials that every Small Group Leader (that's you!) needs to know in order to create an environment in which people can pursue intimacy with God, community with insiders, and influence with outsiders. The essentials are not a checklist for your development as a leader. They're gauges you should monitor, regardless of how long you've been leading.

The first essential is *stay connected*.

Quite often, we as leaders spend so much time and energy on the people we're leading that we get distracted from taking care of ourselves. It's understandable, but it's not sustainable.

We all know that a leader is only as good as the leader whom they are following, but I would go a step further and say that a leader is only as good as the **connection** they have to the leader whom they are following. In John 15, Jesus uses the metaphor of a vine and branches to instruct his followers to "abide" or stay connected to him. Just as the branches are intimately connected to the vine, so you must be intimately connected to Jesus.

We also need to stay connected to relationships that *pour into* us rather than drain us. So be willing to share stories and receive help from your fellow Small Group Leaders, Campus Pastor, or Groups Coach (we're here for you!).

While the people in your group are looking to you to lead them, remember that they are also looking to you to be led well. Stay connected to your Vine, the God who can really change lives. And stay connected to those who pour into you. Make it your top priority to own your spiritual journey, so that you can do the same for others.

Go to https://groupleaders.org/leader-training-feed/2017/2/16/stay-connected#.XEocO6VUIIE to watch a video with more information about Staying Connected.

The Small Group Leaders' Retreat

The winning formula for a leaders' retreat is finding a location a couple of hours out of town and a budget for a speaker with expertise in small groups and/or discipleship. In both churches I served, our retreats were often the weekend after New Year's Day. Most people don't have plans for that weekend, and hotels usually give great rates on their rooms. Our leaders paid for their accommodations and some of their meals, and the church covered the cost of the speaker and some meals. Our leaders from New Life in California would join us in Monterey year after year for this retreat. One couple actually attended seven out of seven retreats!

The schedule for the retreat should balance instruction with time for leaders to connect with one another as well as free time to enjoy the surrounding area. Wearing leaders out with information overload usually isn't helpful, so ask the speaker to address key areas based on their expertise and/or areas of focus for your groups. As a speaker, I've often been asked to challenge leaders with developing leaders, outreach, group multiplication, or other topics pastors wanted their leaders to hear from someone in addition to them (or other than them). Most speakers are open to suggestions.

Sample Retreat Agenda

Friday

4:00–10:00 p.m.	Registration
	Dinner on your own
8:00 p.m.	Welcome and Mixer

Saturday

8:00 a.m.	Breakfast (provided)
9:00 a.m.	Session One with guest speaker
10:15 a.m.	Break
10:30 a.m.	Session Two with guest speaker
12:00 p.m.	Lunch (provided)
1:30 p.m.	Session Three with guest speaker
3:00 p.m.	Free Time
	Dinner on your own

Sunday

8:00 a.m.	Breakfast (provided)
9:00 a.m.	Closing session with guest speaker or senior pastor
11:00 a.m.	Check Out

Enjoy the rest of your day!

After years of trapping people in hotel meeting rooms in beautiful locations to listen to one more lecture and eat delivery pizza in evening sessions, I learned that balance is important (so is feedback!). Here are a couple of other things I've learned about retreat schedules:

- If leaders attend as couples, they might want to have an evening alone, so give them the option.
- Not everyone wants to be alone, so when dinner is "on your own," give an option for people to meet up with you, especially if they are attending the retreat by themselves.
- Group leaders need unscheduled time together. Even though they all lead groups, more than likely they don't know each other. Some of the best memories of a retreat are during the downtime leaders spend together.
- The senior pastor is probably not available to attend the entire retreat, but it's good for your leaders and for your pastor to be involved. (On some retreats, our pastor would speak at the Sunday morning session to close out the retreat. This meant I went back home to preach on that Sunday morning.)

The Best Training

The only way to offer specific, customized training to leaders when they need it is through coaching. I spent most of chapter 10 of *Exponential Groups* building the case for coaching. In this section, I want to build on those thoughts and offer some specifics on leveraging the teachable moments in small group ministry to give appropriate coaching, training, and encouragement to group leaders.

Leaders in different phases of their experience need different things. New leaders need specific direction and support. Experienced leaders need very different things. Think about raising children. Developmental stages are substantially different from infant to toddler to teenager and everything in between. If you treat your teenagers like toddlers, the result is an exponential amount of eye rolling. The same is true of group leaders.

How to Train Different Types of Group Leaders

Let's consider four phases of leader development. This might not be the perfect or exact formula for every group leader and every church, but it provides a framework for a conversation about the diverse needs of group leaders and the coaching they need.

Phase 1: Prospective leaders in their first six-week alignment series. They're in a trial run.

Phase 2: Interested leaders in their second six-week series (follow-up series). They had a good experience leading a group and have decided to continue their groups.

Phase 3: Confirmed leaders in their second semester. At this point, the leader has chosen to lead an on-going group.

Phase 4: Commissioned leaders have completed their first year and have met the requirements for leadership at the church.

If your church doesn't use alignment series, you can substitute "semester" for "series" in this analogy.

Coaching Prospective Leaders (Phase I): New Leaders in Their First Series

Whether these "leaders" are hosting a group in their homes or doing a study with their friends, they are in the trial run with a small group. They have probably never led a group before or conducted a small group meeting. They may have never even attended a group before. These leaders need direction and frequent contacts to succeed.

The New Leader Briefing discussed in chapter 6 gives prospective leaders specific direction about the series, gathering their groups, sharing responsibilities, and connecting with a coach. Since these prospects have not gathered a group or led a meeting before, the instructions are simple and direct and the coaching contacts are frequent. I recommend weekly phone calls from the coach to keep the prospective leaders encouraged and motivate as they gather their groups and lead for the first time. They will have a lot of questions as they get started, so the frequent interactions with their coaches are essential for their success.

Now, let's look at the other side of the equation. Not only are leaders being developed but coaches are also being developed along with them. To successfully coach prospective leaders, coaches need to understand how to start a new group—preferably by having started and led a group themselves. Coaches could even be called upon to deliver all or part of the New Leader Briefing. They are expected to be able to answer all of the basic questions from their new leaders by drawing on their own experience and any resources provided to them. Coaching at this phase relies on the coach's ability to encourage leaders. The goal of coaching in Phase 1 is to start the first study and then encourage the leaders and groups to continue into the next step study (chapter 8).

Coaches at this point are best equipped with their own experience. Most coaches with some experience can address questions from new leaders. These coaches might also benefit from one of the books I mentioned earlier in the chapter, especially *Making Small Groups Work* or *Leading Healthy Groups*, which both offer a ready reference for common small group issues. They can also consult chapter 9 of *Exponential Groups*. These coaches will report to either a small group team member in a church with over a thousand in attendance or the small group pastor in a church under a thousand. If there are any questions they cannot answer or more serious issues that might arise in a group, these should be brought to the person supervising them.

Coaching Interested Leaders (Phase 2): New Leaders in Their Second Series

This phase of coaching is one of the most important steps in the development of a leader and group. At this point, the leader has successfully completed the trial run of an alignment series and has chosen to do the next step study. Most new leaders in this phase will continue on the pathway toward becoming a commissioned leader.

In Phase 2, coaches want to see their leaders sharing responsibilities with their group members as part of developing future leaders (*EG* 184–85). At this point, leaders know their way around a group meeting and are probably feeling more confident about leading. These are great milestones, considering that only six weeks before, these folks weren't even sure they had what it took to be a group leader.

The goal for a leader now is to complete the second study and then commit to a longer term as a group leader. The coach can begin to mention some of the resources like Basic Training (chapter 9) that are available to leaders, but they should avoid pushing too much too fast. The church wants to avoid these new leaders going underground.

Training should be delivered as group leaders need it. After spending six to twelve weeks together, some group issues will begin to surface. Group members will begin to notice the differences among them, which may become a source of irritation. A few people will talk too much, while others will whisper to their neighbors rather than share with the group. Some folks will consistently show up late, and some might even try to dominate the group with their problems. As these issues appear, the coach should guide the leader on how to manage these group dynamics. Again, this is not the place for a meeting to frontload a ton of training on group dynamics. But these are things to watch for and address as the issues surface. Some groups will have more issues than others, while other groups may not appear to have any issues . . . yet.

The beauty of coaching is that specific help can be delivered for specific issues. And if coaches are new to coaching, they can learn right along with the group leaders. If the coaches are aware of issues but unsure of how to handle them, the coaches can study group resources and/or talk to their supervisors before making a recommendation to the group leaders. While it may be awkward for coaches to admit they don't know something, searching for an answer will actually build their credibility with the leaders. They will see that the coaches care enough to seek out a good answer rather than just shoot from the hip.

At this point, coaches can reduce the number of regular contacts with the leaders from weekly to every other week. Having the experience of leading a study already, group leaders need less direction than they did in the first series. If group leaders have an issue, they can always contact their coach.

This might also be the opportunity for coaches to visit groups, if they haven't already. If the group has an issue the coach needs to observe, then the visit should happen sooner rather than later. But the other side of this is that some leaders won't realize they have issues in their groups until a coach points them out.

The group visit should be scheduled in advance with the group leader, and the group should know a guest is coming. A successful group visit starts with the coach arriving before the group members arrive. The coach should ask the group leader if there is anything the coach should pay special attention to during the group meeting.

As the group members arrive, the coach should just blend in and participate like any other group member in the meeting. They can make notes in the study guide about anything they observe in the group or just make mental notes. Coaches certainly shouldn't sit in the corner filling out a form on a clipboard. (Unfortunately, I've done that. Talk about the principal showing up.) At some point in the meeting, it would be appropriate for the coach to briefly address the group. The coach's goal in the group meeting is to build up the leader, to build up the study, and to build up the church.

After the meeting, the coach should stay behind until all the group members have left. Once the coach is alone with the leader, they should then discuss what the coach observed in the meeting and explore possible solutions for any issues that might have surfaced in the meeting. While some issues might be resolved simply with just one conversation, other problems might take more time and additional coaching visits.

One side note: If coaches also lead their own groups, it's important for the coach to have a co-leader. This will enable coaches to visit groups even if a meeting conflicts with the coach's own group meeting. It will also keep busy coaches from becoming overloaded in their responsibilities for their own groups and for other group leaders.

As the coaches are helping their leaders navigate group dynamics and other issues, they should be equipped with resources for referrals. They should know what support groups and counselors are available through the church or in the community. They should also be aware of what pastoral care, counseling, and financial assistance is offered at the church. (To know when to refer group members to resources outside of the group, see *EG* 195–97.)

Again, the goal of Phase 2 is to help these new leaders continue down the pathway toward become a commissioned leader (Phase 4). Leaders should be offered what they need when they need it. But at this point, leadership requirements should be suggested, not mandated.

Coaching Confirmed Leaders (Phase 3): New Leaders in Their Second Semester

Confirmed leaders in Phase 3 are one step closer to being "official." Some of these may have already completed the leadership pathway. Most probably haven't yet.

The role of a group leader is not merely running group meetings or even leading a group. The purpose of groups is discipleship. Disciples make disciples. This is the mission Jesus gave to the church in Matthew 28:18–20:

> Then Jesus came to them and said, "All authority in heaven and on earth has been given to me. Therefore go and make disciples of all nations, baptizing them in the name of the Father and of the Son and of the Holy Spirit, and teaching them to obey everything I have commanded you. And surely I am with you always, to the very end of the age."

From this passage, the instructions are given to "go," which points to the group's need to reach out to others. The task is to "make disciples." In examining Jesus' method of developing his twelve disciples, he used a combination of commitment, time together, sending them out, serving together, teaching, correction, leadership development, and risk.

Every disciple including every group leader has the same mission to go and make disciples. The clear direction from Matthew 28 on making a disciple is to baptize them and teach them to obey. Baptism is a public acknowledgement of belonging to Jesus. It's a visible sign of the work of salvation that is expressed in different ways in different churches. This is not the place for debate on how or when someone should be baptized, but disciples should be baptized.

Next, Jesus instructs his disciples to teach their disciples to obey (v. 20). Although this is different from teaching lessons and principles, it could include this. The reality is that just because people know what to do something does not mean they will do it. Without becoming heavy-handed or legalistic, Jesus commands his disciples to teach their disciples to obey "everything I have commanded you." How is this done practically?

Teaching disciples to obey starts with the idea of believing Jesus meant what he said. When groups explore the Sermon on the Mount (Matthew 5–7), his parables, and other teaching, the group takes Jesus' words seriously and expresses an openness to do something about what they've heard. (This also applies to the rest of Scripture's teaching.)

Obedience to Jesus' commands starts with the group members' intention, which is best expressed in a goal. In the application section of a study or toward the end of the meeting, each group member should set a goal or take on an assignment they will try to achieve in the next week with both God's help and the group's support. By stating a goal, the group member begins down the path of obedience.

The group can support each member's goals by offering encouragement and accountability. This might involve groups of two or three members supporting one another, perhaps reminding one another throughout the week. In the next meeting, group members should then be asked about their progress in reaching their goal. Accountability does not need to be heavy-handed. Often knowing someone will ask the question will motivate the group member to accomplish their goal for the week. Some goals might be larger or multipart and will take a longer time to achieve; group members should be patient with each other and continue to "spur one another on toward love and good deeds" (Hebrews 10:24). The emphasis is not on lessons learned but on lessons lived.

Coaches can play a role by doing for the group leaders what the leaders are supposed to do for their group members—that is, encourage and support them in their spiritual next steps and offer appropriate accountability. While every believer has a spiritual next step, sometimes group leaders don't want to address their next steps, sinful behavior, or past hurts with their groups. This is where a coach can help to facilitate growth and healing in the leaders' lives.

In this phase, the group leader's role shifts. In addition to the responsibility of meetings, the leader should set the tone for spiritual growth in the group by keeping the principles of making disciples in front of the group members, both through the group meetings as well as the leader's own participation. The goal is to help every group member grow as a disciple.

Leaders will also see some of their group members rise to the top, so to speak. By sharing responsibilities, some members will demonstrate ability to possibly lead their own groups. They should be given opportunity to develop their leadership skills in the group. They could lead all or part of group meetings. They could also plan social activities or service projects for the group. Before the idea of group leadership is floated to a prospective leader, however, the group leaders should discuss the choice with their coaches to determine whether this is a wise decision. If the prospect is approved, then the group leader should encourage the new leader to lead a group of their own—maybe for the next alignment series.

At this stage of coaching and leader development, the coaches' primary role should shift from giving answers to asking questions. At this point, most group leaders know what to do. They know how to lead a meeting. They know how to handle many of the dynamics going on in the group. The coaches' approach needs to shift from telling to asking. (Details on the use of asking and interviews in coaching can be found in *EG* chapter 10.) The frequency of contacts can decrease from every other week to once per month or even once per quarter depending on how much help the leaders need.

The goal at this point is to encourage the group leader toward becoming a commissioned leader (Phase 4). Basic Training, as described in chapter 9, should be offered at this point by invitation. Other requirements that might have been delayed can now begin to be discussed. This could include church membership, a growth track, or other parts of the church's leader development process. Avoid mandating these requirements at this point. After all, you attract more flies with honey . . .

While there might be hesitation to put more requirements or responsibilities on group leaders, the reality is that leaders need to be developed in order to produce healthy leaders and groups. If the requirements remain low, then the church is communicating that leading a group is not very important because anyone can do it. By bringing back the requirements that were once delayed and turning up the temperature on discipleship, healthy groups will become environments where disciples make disciples.

Coaching Commissioned Leaders (Phase 4): Leaders Who Have Led for One Year or More

Commissioned leaders have met all of the church's leadership requirements and have been officially recognized as small group leaders by the church. This is the church's hope for every potential leader who gathers a group for an alignment series. At this point, Phase 4 leaders have a good grasp on small group leadership and don't need a great deal of personal attention. While some contact should be maintained, the need should have lessened considerably unless there is an issue going on with the group. As always, coaches should be available for all of their leaders and any situations that come up. At this point, it's just as important for coaches to know when to back off as it is to know when to intervene.

In Phase 4, the focus continues in helping leaders identify and take their own personal next steps. The group leaders' purpose advances in making disciples and equipping group members to lead at various levels. If any group members have left the group to start their own groups, then their group leader would be the logical choice to coach them since they already have a relationship. Coaching their former group members who now lead is an honor for small group leaders.

The designations of these four phases serve to emphasize that leaders need different coaching at different points in their growth as leaders and as disciples themselves. Coaching is customizable to the leaders' needs and interests. New leaders need more direction and instruction while leading their first couple of studies, and leaders who have led for a while don't need as much attention. In fact, they might resent any perceived over-involvement by the coach. When leaders are more experienced, they need coaches to designate time to help them process what's going on in their groups. They don't need to be told what to do; they need the coach to ask questions and offer support and accountability.

Coaches need to grow along with their leaders. Since coaching is built on a relationship, it would make sense for coaches and leaders to continue their relationship, as long as the coaches can adapt to their leaders' changing needs. If a coach proves to be more of a teacher or instructor than a coach or mentor, then that coach would better serve new leaders and hand off experienced leaders to another coach when they reach Phase 3.

Do New Things with New Leaders

Although this has been mentioned elsewhere, it bears repeating. If the church does not currently offer coaching to its group leaders, then it should start with the new leaders only. New leaders will be far more accepting of a coach than experienced leaders typically are. It's okay not to have every space filled in on the organizational chart initially. Start with new leaders because they need the most help. Don't feel guilty about experienced leaders who have not received coaching. They are your best prospects for coaching. They've figured it out.

As experienced leaders coach new leaders, the person they report to (a small group pastor or team member) essentially becomes their coach. From the experience of coaching others, these seasoned leaders will begin to understand the benefit of having a coach.

Coaching Assignments

Since coaching begins with a relationship, coaches should partner up with new group leaders they already know. If coaches are meeting their new leaders at a New Leader Briefing, then encourage them to scan the room to see who they already know. At the end of the briefing, ask coaches to make a beeline directly to the new leaders they already know and agree to become their coach.

If coaches are responsible for a particular affinity (Men's Groups, Women's Groups, Couples' Groups, Singles' Groups, and so on) or are responsible for a geographical region and they don't know any of the new leaders at the briefing, they should partner with the leaders who align with their area of responsibility.

Due to the nature of the coaching relationship, it's best for new leaders to have a coach of the same gender. An alternative is a model where the coaches work as married couples and coach new leaders together.

Exercise: Leadership Phases

Write the group leaders' names in the appropriate phase.

Phase 1: Prospective Leaders (in First Series)	Phase 2: Interested Leaders (in Follow-Up Series)	Phase 3: Confirmed Leaders (in Second Semester)	Phase 4: Commissioned Leaders (in Second Year)

▶ Case Study ◀

Rivertown Community Church

Rivertown Community Church in Marianna, Florida, has been led by Senior Pastor Paul Smith for twenty-seven years. It has about 1,400 adults weekly across five campuses in the Florida Panhandle. The church currently has a hundred small groups.

After several attempts at developing a coaching structure, the church became frustrated. "I've been on staff for thirteen years," said Kevin Yoder, campus pastor. "We probably looked at about four rounds of trying to introduce coaches over small group leaders. Our efforts immediately fell flat. We tried to bring a bunch of coaches in at one time. We tried to onboard a larger coaching structure than what was really needed. The coaches ended up having so few leaders with such differing backgrounds that there was really no synergy. Nothing really took off."

While the spirit of the church to support their group leaders with coaches was good, they struggled with building too much too soon. Smaller campuses with just a handful of groups did not need the elaborate structure that the larger campuses required. The other struggle involved how to coach different leaders. For the most part, all of the leaders were coached exactly the same regardless of their experience or skill as leaders.

"The concept of the four phases of leader development helped me understand how to coach leaders at different stages of their journey in leading small groups," Yoder said. "As we evaluated our leaders, it was clear that this leader is in this phase and that leader is in a different phase and has different needs. It gave our coaches the freedom to move away from a one-size-fits-all mentality."

The coaching model provided the scalability a growing church with multiple campuses needed for a growing small group ministry. Smaller campuses with five or so groups needed only their campus pastor to coach the leaders, but bearing in mind that a coach or two might be needed in the near future. A campus of ninety adults had different needs from the largest campus of eight hundred people.

As the number of leaders increased, coaches were added on a trial run basis at first. "As you say," Yoder told me, "we asked ourselves who the leaders were that we wanted more of. We invited them to informally coach or mentor another leader for one season to see how the leader responded and how the coach responded. That helped us confirm or negate that coach's ability." Some coaches succeeded. "One lady who was a new coach worked with another leader and did a fabulous job. So, we're bringing her on as a coach for the next semester." There were others who did not do so well and didn't make the cut. This is the advantage of a trial run experience.

To reinforce the relationship between the coaches and their group leaders, the church provided talking points for the coaches to discuss with the leaders. These talking points ensured that the information from the church was delivered and helped the coaches by requiring less preparation time. "We really wanted to reinforce the relationship of the leader and the coach. We wanted the leader to see the coach as the one helping to guide them. We gave the coaches and campus pastors tools to pass on to the leaders."

In a church of any size, the beauty of a coaching structure is that most of the issues that come up in groups can be addressed by a coach. This frees up pastors and staff for other ministry work, and it develops group leaders into mentors who serve other groups leaders. "Sometimes the coaches bring issues to me, but this is very seldom. Even when those issues arise, I coach the coach on how to handle the situation." The leaders and groups are well served through coaching.

Coaching Thresholds

Since most coaches will also lead their own small groups, it's important not to overwhelm coaches with too many of the same type of small group leaders. New leaders need more help, so how many new leaders can a coach be available for? More mature leaders in the later phases don't need as much time and attention. The point here is that each coach should have a balance of leader types. Coaching capacity depends on the coach's ability and availability. If the church does not currently offer coaching to its leaders, then the focus is on coaching new leaders only. As those leaders grow and mature, other new leaders could be added to a coach's responsibility. As stated before, coaches also need to be able to grow as a coach as their leaders grow in their abilities. Can the coach be directive with new leaders, and then back off and be more supportive to experienced leaders? If experienced leaders are treated like new leaders, it will be bad for everyone.

With this in mind, what is the appropriate mix of group leaders for a coach? Granted, each coach's relational ability and availability are different. Some coaches may be brilliant with three leaders but a disaster coaching four leaders. Supervising coaches is important to make sure they don't become overloaded. Don't expect the same capacity from every coach.

Consider the Frequency of Contacts for Different Types of Leaders

With this in mind, how many new leaders can each coach handle? How many Phase 4 leaders? How many in Phase 1? Each coach needs the right balance to fit their ability and availability. Consider how many contacts will be required of a coach over a twelve-week period.

Phase 1: Prospective Leaders (in 1st Series)	Phase 2: Interested Leaders (in Follow-up Series)	Phase 3: Confirmed Leaders (in 2nd Semester)	Phase 4: Commissioned Leaders (in 2nd Year)
Weekly Contacts	Every Other Week Contacts	Monthly Contacts	Quarterly Contacts
9 Contacts in 12 Weeks (Weekly for 6 weeks, then every other week for 6 weeks)	4–5 Contacts in 12 Weeks (Every other week for 6 weeks, then monthly for 6 weeks)	3 Contacts in 12 Weeks	1 Contact in 12 Weeks

A coach with three Phase 1 leaders will make twenty-seven contacts in the first twelve weeks, whereas a coach with three Phase 3 leaders will make only nine contacts in the same time period. The point is not to load up a coach with all new leaders, except for the first time around, but even then a new coach should only have two or three new leaders at the most. Over time, keep the balance between the four phases of leaders.

The big point I want for you to take away from this chapter is that the more specific training you can offer to individual leaders, the more effective your training will be. While there are some macro issues that will apply to all group leaders—such as casting vision for groups, developing new leaders, informing about upcoming series, and so forth—the most meaningful training is delivered when the leader faces the actual situation. Educators call this a teachable moment. When the student is interested and asks questions, this is when the lesson is best learned. Coaching is a big part of this. Also, on demand training can supplement the coach's insights. But hear this: Put your work into coaching before you develop a video training library. Often small group pastors can become enamored with techie solutions, but human solutions are superior.

Chapter 11

Tracking Growth

Not many leaders get excited about reports. After all, leadership is soaring with the eagles. Management and reports feels more like clucking with the chickens. But without data, leaders can only guess.

I believe there are three major categories in small group ministry that deserve tracking: (1) Group Rosters and Attendance, (2) Leader Development and Coaching, and (3) Group Member Spiritual Growth. If the church uses a comprehensive database, such as ChurchTeams.com, most of these reports will be generated automatically from the coach and leader input.

When it comes to data, however, numbers tell only part of the story. There are both hard and soft metrics to consider. It's one thing to know how many people regularly attend a group, and it's another to know what God is doing in the lives of the group members. Both types are important to see the whole picture of what's working and what's not working with groups.

Group Rosters and Attendance

In chapter 11 of *Exponential Groups*, there are reasons—both good and bad—for keeping attendance for groups. The bottom line is that small group pastors should track whatever numbers the people they report to require, and then there might be a few other numbers small group pastors want to follow as well.

Rosters provide a way to know who is in a group and who is not. The hope is that those who are not in groups would eventually join a group and that those in a group are growing spiritually and being developed into leaders. Accurate lists are the only way to know what's going on. As with any other type of data, of course, group rosters are essentially "garbage in, garbage out." Reports are only as good as the data given.

As a group begins, the roster should be collected in one of a variety of ways: paper form, database entries, or online survey. The paper form can be as simple as the Connection Event sign-up sheet (see page 87 in this workbook). At Brookwood Church, the print shop actually made a two-part form. One copy went home with the group leader, and the other was collected by church staff.

Online survey tools allow group leaders to share their group member list, enabling the church to download the list in a digital file. Surveys can be used to collect group rosters at the beginning of an alignment series, gauge the group leader's intention to continue the group in the middle of the series, and receive feedback about the series and the church's self-produced curriculum.

Sample Survey to Collect Group Roster at Beginning of Series

1. List the names of everyone who has committed to your group or attended the first meeting.

2. What is one question about your group we haven't answered yet?

3. Were you in a small group or Bible study last year?   ☐ Yes   ☐ No

4. If you were in a small group before, what capacity did you serve in? (Use Skip Logic)

    ☐ Small Group Leader
    ☐ Small Group Co-leader
    ☐ Small Group Host
    ☐ Event Coordinator (social, serving, outreach, or other)
    ☐ Small Group Member
    ☐ Other, please describe: _____

Some churches will ask for more information about their leaders through a beginning of the serie survey like this; but if the church has hosted a briefing, most of the information should have been provided by the group leaders on the Leader Information Sheet (page 74).

Databases such as ChurchTeams.com are easy to use and allow group leaders themselves to input their rosters and group information online. Some databases require a great deal of personal information including birth dates, contact information, or other more extensive information that must be entered and/or approved by church office staff. If a group is in its first alignment series, which means the group may or may not continue, or if the church database requires more than the group members' names and e-mail addresses, then I would recommend tracking these groups on a spreadsheet for the first alignment series. Once the group has indicated it will move forward into the follow-up series and beyond, then the group leaders and church staff can do the hard work of setting up the groups in the church database.

If the database is easy for the leaders to input the information themselves, then the new groups could certainly be entered even in the first series. If groups are "Invitation Only" as described in chapter 3, then these groups should not be made public in a church database. A good database should allow the church to show or hide groups depending on their status.

Tracking group attendance can be tricky without a good online tool. Submitting weekly paper forms or sending weekly surveys is cumbersome. One of the best features of ChurchTeams.com is its group reporting function. Each week after the meeting, the group leader or designated report-taker receives an e-mail requesting the report. (Reports in this section are used with the permission of ChurchTeams.com).

The group leader simply clicks the appropriate response about their group meeting, and then is securely taken to the reporting page without having to login to the database. The report can be given on a smartphone, tablet, or computer.

Meeting Report Reminder

Meeting Report Form

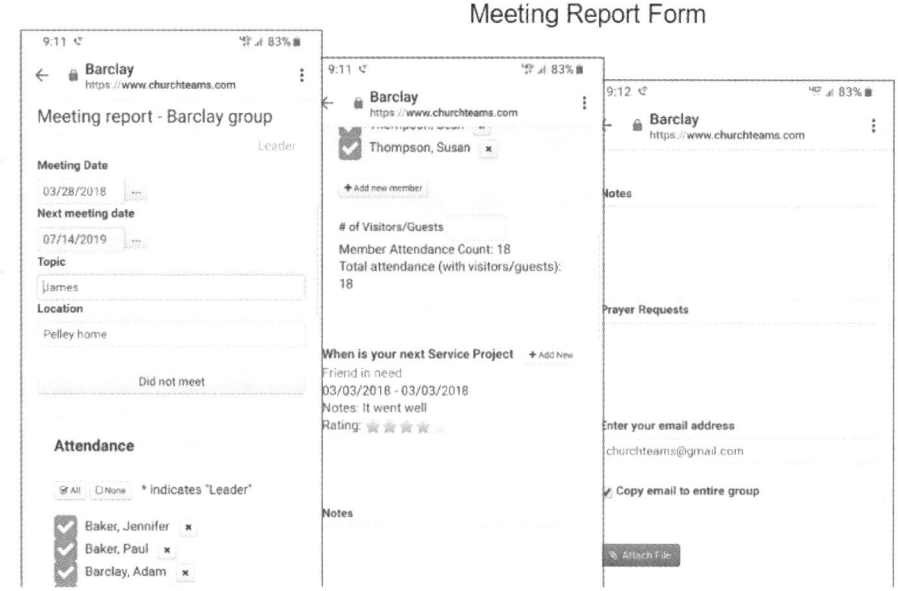

A weekly group report should ask for the meeting date, attendance, any notes about the meeting, and prayer requests from the group. This report should be shared with the group leader's coach, small group pastor, relevant church staff, and others the church designates.

In ChurchTeams, this information is automatically e-mailed to those designated to receive the report immediately after the group leader submits the report. If the church database does not include this feature, below is an example of the type of report the coach, small group team, and small group pastor should receive for each group on a weekly basis. Even in churches with dozens or hundreds or thousands of groups, this information is important to ensure the care of group members and to support group leaders in serving their groups. Ignorance is not bliss when group members are struggling.

Reports should be analyzed for trends. Is the group growing dramatically? Is the group noticeably shrinking? Is the group meeting consistently? Are group members attending consistently? Have any group members dropped out? The church database should be able to calculate this information.

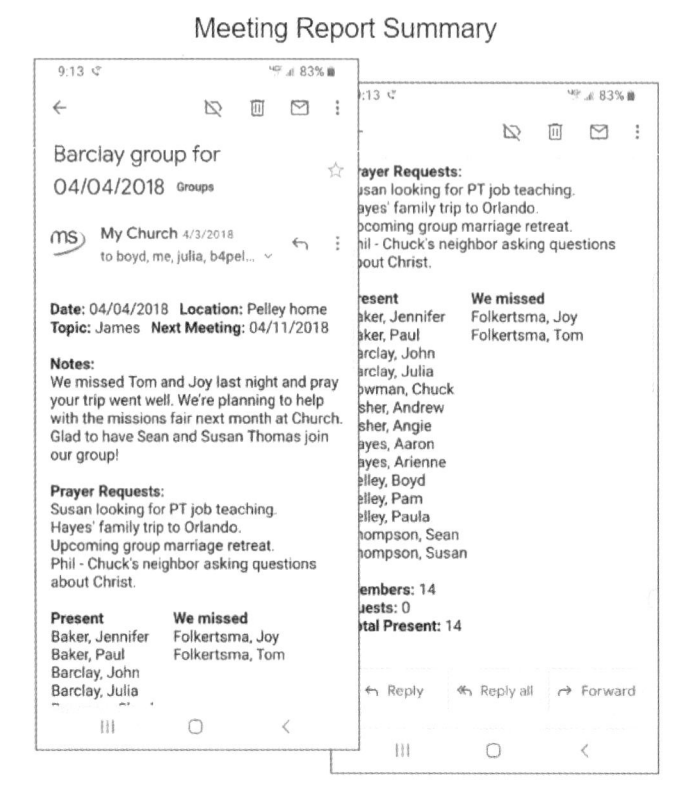

Meeting Report Summary

Group Name	Enrollment	05/27-06/02	06/03-06/09	06/10-06/16	06/17-06/23	06/24-06/30	# of Meetings	Avg #	Avg %
Clark Group	8	NR	NR	NR	NR	NR	0		0.0%
Hoak	12	5	4	5	4	NR	4	4.5	37.5%
Cunningham	10	3	5	4	4	NR	4	4.0	40.0%
Delano	4	DNM	2	DNM	2	NR	2	2.0	50.0%
Johnson	11	6	6	6	6	NR	4	6.0	54.5%
Garcia Men	7	5	NMS	4	4	NR	3	4.3	61.9%
Young Singles	8	5	5	DNM	5	NR	3	5.0	62.5%
Lovejoy	9	6	6	7	6	NR	4	6.3	69.4%
Mildred	6	4	4	5	4	NR	4	4.3	70.8%
Fadely	7	5	5	5	6	NR	4	5.3	75.0%
Barclay	14	15	16	12	13	2	5	11.6	82.9%
Niner	12	10	10	10	10	NR	4	10.0	83.3%
Garcia	7	6	6	6	6	NR	4	6.0	85.7%
Thompson	11	10	10	10	10	NR	4	10.0	90.9%
Roberts	10	10	9	10	10	NR	4	9.8	97.5%
Late Night	4	4	DNM	4	4	NR	3	4.0	100.0%
Jackson	7	8	7	7	7	NR	4	7.3	103.6%
Facebook Link	5	6	DNM	6	6	NR	3	6.0	120.0%
Guest only totals	8	3	2	1	2	0		1.6	
Distinct Members	85	67	65	66	70	2			
Total Expected Attendance		140	128	132	144	14	558	112	
Totals for Life Group	152	108	95	101	107	2	413	82.6	106.2
# of Groups Meeting		16	14	15	17	1			
% Groups that met		88.9%	77.8%	83.3%	94.4%	5.6%			
Attendance % Enrolled		77.1%	74.2%	76.5%	74.3%	14.3%			74.0%
# of Groups	18								
Total Enrollment	152								

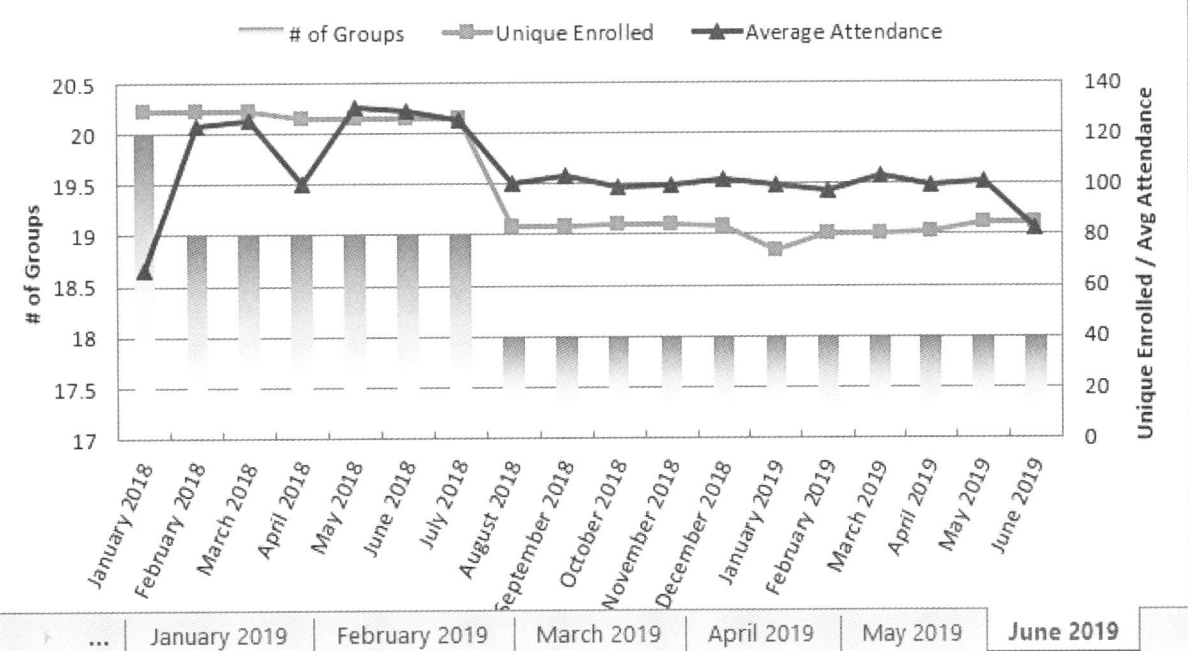

Group / Enrollment History for Life Group

| … | January 2019 | February 2019 | March 2019 | April 2019 | May 2019 | June 2019 |

Attendance by Member Consistency					

04/29/2019 to 05/26/2019
People in group
Groups: 'Barclay'
Active Groups

DNM = Did not meet — Healthy: 80%+
NMS = No meeting scheduled — Normal: 50 - 79%
NR = Not reported — Stress: 0 - 50%
X = Attended

Barclay	04/29 - 05/05	05/06 - 05/12	05/13 - 05/19	05/20 - 05/26	
Abad, Phyllis				X	25%
Garrett, Cash				X	25%
Pelley, Boyd				X	25%
Seawell, James				X	25%
Fisher, Andrew		X	X	X	75%
Fisher, Angie		X	X	X	75%
Folkertsma, Joy	X		X	X	75%
Folkertsma, Tom	X	X	X		75%
Hayes, Arienne	X	X	X		75%
Barclay, Adam	X	X	X	X	100%
Barclay, Julia	X	X	X	X	100%
Hayes, Aaron	X	X	X	X	100%
Thomas, Emily	X	X	X	X	100%
Thomas, Eric	X	X	X	X	100%
# of Group Members	11	12	14	14	
# of Attendees	8	9	10	12	
	72.7%	75%	71.4%	85.7%	Overall Percentage: 76.4%

Distinct members attending at least once: 14
Distinct members attending twice or more: 10

A monthly report summary for all of the groups can help coaches, the small group team, and the small group pastor identify which groups are succeeding and which groups might be struggling.

Leader Development and Coaching

The church must track what is important to the growth and future development of the small group ministry. The purpose is not to get bogged down in management functions, but rather to ask for accountability in what the church believes is important and to make sure these things are happening. If the church says that leader development is important, yet doesn't ask the groups to report on how they are developing leaders, then the perception is that leader development is not important, because no one asks about it.

If the church believes it's important for small groups to share leadership responsibilities in the group to develop new leaders, then a survey question should be included to identify what the groups are doing. Here is a sample question:

> **During this study, which of the following did your group do?**
> **(check all that apply)**

☐ Different members led the group meeting

☐ Different members led a portion of the group meeting (icebreaker, prayer time, etc.)

☐ Different members hosted the group in their home

☐ Different members brought refreshments to the meetings

- ☐ A member(s) of the group led a sub-group(s) during the group meetings
- ☐ One or more group members planned a service project for the group
- ☐ One or more group members planned a group social
- ☐ One or more group members planned an outreach event or open house for the group
- ☐ The group designated a co-leader or apprentice
- ☐ The group is planning to start another group

As someone once said, you have to inspect what you expect. Leadership development happens when vision is cast, and vision is reinforced through repeated messages and coaching conversations, plans are made, and accountability is provided. By not asking about progress in leadership development, the church is communicating that either they weren't serious about groups sharing leadership or that leadership development is really not important.

Coaching Reports

The same is true of coaching. If the church has coaches in place to support, encourage, and train leaders, then the church should monitor how this is being done. Years ago, author and church consultant Carl George shared with a group of small group pastors I was part of that the health of small groups could be predicted by the frequency of contacts between the coaches and group leaders.[14] Coaching contacts are important, so they must be treated as important by asking for coaches to report on their involvement with groups.

Please understand, I don't personally get excited about report-taking or analyzing them. In my heart of hearts, I would rather just hope everything is going well and not even ask. But execution without validation is fiction. As hard as it might be to ask for reports, the lack of accountability can be devastating to a small group coaching structure. Below are some sample coaching reports generated by ChurchTeams.com.

Coaching Report Form

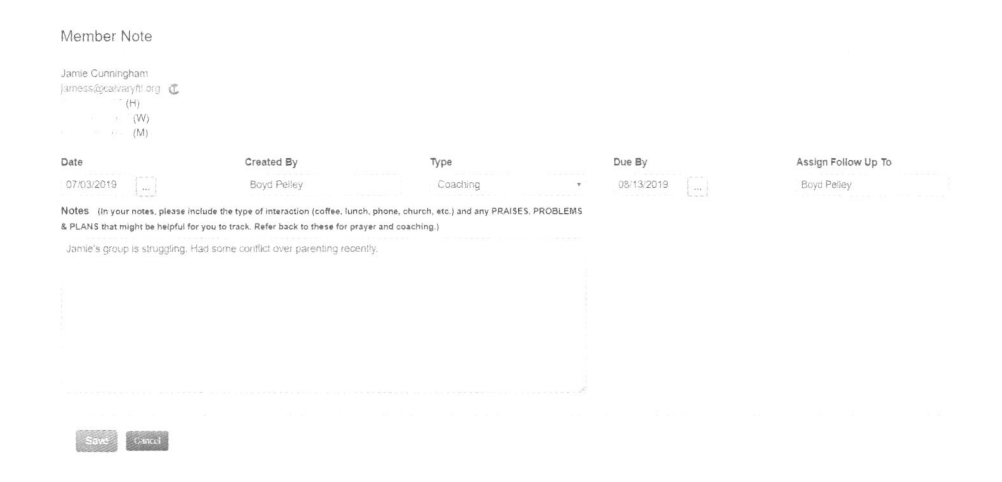

A summary document like the one below is significant to determine which group leaders have been contacted and which have not. Again, this is not paperwork for the sake of paperwork. A monthly contact report that includes the results of the contact or the reality of no contact being made will help in the care of small group leaders. This report can be delivered in various formats—paper document, e-mail, survey, etc. The following reports for an individual team member responsible for specific coaches, as well as a general report for the church for all coaches, were generated by ChurchTeams.com based on the coach input.

Coaching summary for My Church

My Church <groupfinder@churchteams.com>
to boyd, mark, me

Coaching summary for My Church:

50% (1/2) of the Leaders under **"Staff" John Barclay** were contacted by their Coach in the last month.
50% (1/2) of the Leaders were contacted by their Coach in the last two months.
Those not contacted in last two months are:
Young Singles group under Gene Bikis
63.2% (12/19) of the Leaders under **"Staff" Boyd Pelley** were contacted by their Coach in the last month.
94.7% (18/19) of the Leaders were contacted by their Coach in the last two months.
Those not contacted in last two months are:
Thompson group under Boyd Pelley

Overall 61.9% (13/21) of the Leaders were contacted by their Coach in the last month.
90.5% (19/21) of the Leaders were contacted by their Coach in the last two months.

Coaching summary for My Church   Inbox x

My Church
to me, mark, churchteams

Coaching summary for My Church:

0% (0/2) of the Leaders under **"Staff" Adam Barclay** were contacted by their Coach in the last month
0% (0/2) of the Leaders were contacted by their Coach in the last two months
Those not contacted in last two months are:
Dyer group under Gene Bikis
Young Singles group under Gene Bikis
31.6% (6/19) of the Leaders under **"Staff" Boyd Pelley** were contacted by their Coach in the last month
31.6% (6/19) of the Leaders were contacted by their Coach in the last two months
Those not contacted in last two months are:
Garcia group under Andrew Fisher
Jackson group under Andrew Fisher
Dresden group under Macy Kuykendall
Barclay group under Boyd Pelley
Emerson group under Boyd Pelley
Cunningham group under Boyd Pelley
Phillips group under Boyd Pelley
Lamb group under Boyd Pelley

Overall 28.6% (6/21) of the Leaders were contacted by their Coach in the last month.
28.6% (6/21) of the Leaders were contacted by their Coach in the last two months.

The primary purpose of coaching is supporting group leaders, not report-taking or report-giving. Conversations between coaches and leaders should not devolve into "Have you completed your report?" The same is true in conversations between small group pastors and coaches. This is why I strongly advocate for effective online tools with automatic report requests to take the hassle out of reporting. If the church is unable to provide such a database tool, then paper reports, e-mails, or surveys can serve as substitutes. Church members could be asked to volunteer their time for data processing and report analysis. It's never a bad thing to ask more people to get their gifts into the game.

Group Member Spiritual Growth

Spiritual growth is probably the most difficult thing to measure. While it's easy to measure meetings attended, lessons learned, and verses memorized, it's more challenging to measure the impact these meetings, lessons, and verses have had on changing attitudes and actions. Even though these metrics are difficult to acquire, this is the church's most important work. The church's mission is to make disciples. If the church is not making disciples, then what is it making?

Several measurement tools are available to gauge members' growth. Instruments like these should be used to receive a base measurement, and then repeated annually to see how each person as well as the church as a whole has grown. Here are a few assessments to track spiritual growth:

- *The Christian Life Profile Assessment Tool* by Randy Frazee
- REVEAL for Church and for Individuals
- *Spiritual Health Assessment and Spiritual Health Planner* by Saddleback Church
- *The Spiritual Assessment Inventory: A Theistic Model and Measure for Assessing Spiritual Development* by Todd Hall and Keith Edwards
- GroupFinder by ChurchTeams.com

The church can also develop its own assessment tool by writing four or five questions related to each of the church's stated values. Members can then be asked to rate themselves on a scale of what they believe, what they think, and what they do.:

No matter what method a church uses, assessing the spiritual growth of its members and the church as a whole is important in order to know how well the church is succeeding in fulfilling its mission and reaching its goals. Most churches can measure services conducted, events, attendance, giving, and even how many people are connected into groups, but what impact are these things having on the individual members of the church? Where do members need training and information? Where do they need motivation and accountability? A spiritual growth assessment provides metrics to determine where the church needs to apply its effort to reach its goals or even how the church might need to adjust its goals.

Gathering Soft Metrics through Storytelling

Hard metrics give only part of the picture of what is taking place with groups and growth in a church. The other part of the picture comes from the soft metrics of storytelling. What is God doing in the lives of individual group members? What is changing in them? How is the group impacting them? How are they overcoming life's challenges?

Storytelling is important to fully understand the impact the church is having on its members. Stories are also a powerful tool to cast vision for the church, groups, and spiritual growth. Going back to the *Diffusion of Innovations* research (cited in *EG* chapter 8), the first step in adopting a new idea is information. This is what churches deliver from their pulpits, websites, and brochures about groups and growth. The second step is persuasion. More often than not, persuasion comes from members telling other members about their experiences in groups. Another dimension of persuasion is recording members' stories to use as promotional videos or sermon illustrations about groups. Stories cast vision.

Stories can be collected by asking group leaders who has been impacted by their groups. This can be conveyed in coaching conversations or through reports. Group leaders and even members can be asked to share their stories in writing through a bulletin insert, a survey, or some other means to hear what God has done in their lives through their group or through a particular study. Some of these members could be selected to elaborate on their written stories and even tell their stories on video.

Stories are not only powerful to cast vision to the congregation, but they are also significant in affirming the pastors, staff, coaches, and others who have worked hard to create and sustain groups in their churches. Once stories are collected, make sure you receive permission to share them. Then you can e-mail stories to group leaders. Give the stories to senior pastors to build their confidence in groups. Tell the world what God is doing!

Hard and soft metrics together paint a fuller picture of the state of discipleship in a church. For some, collecting and analyzing reports is about as exciting as filing income taxes. But reports are significant. They are an accounting for the lives with which the church has been entrusted. People need to connect with other believers in order to grow. In order to form a group, there must be a leader. How are leaders being developed? How are leaders supported? And when it's all said and done, what impact has all of this had in helping members obey all that Jesus commanded and make disciples themselves?

Chapter 12

Beyond Alignment Series

Once a church has successfully connected its regular members and attendees into groups, it's time then to move beyond alignment series. The first widely publicized church-wide campaign, the *40 Days of Purpose* by Rick Warren, was launched in 2002. By far, it has been the most popular campaign to date. I am grateful for every person who ever "hosted" or joined a group for that season.

At this point, some of you may be confused. The *Exponential Groups* book and this workbook are all about alignment series. Some might ask, "Now you're telling us that campaigns don't work." That's not what I'm saying. Although alignment series do work, there is a time and a season for them. Here are the reasons for those seasons.

When to Stop Using Alignment Series

There are two measures for when alignment series are no longer effective. When the church hits these marks, then alignments will no longer be helpful.

First, if a high percentage of the church's members are in groups, it no longer needs to use alignment series. For most churches, there is a one- to three-year window when alignments are highly effective to recruit leaders and connect people into groups. Beyond that window, the church will experience "campaign fatigue." It's a strange phenomenon.

Every week, people will hear a message in the weekend service. Every week, people will meet in their groups and probably study something. But the idea of continually aligning the weekend service with the group study gets exhausting for people. While this may seem strange since there is a sermon and a study every week, it's a reality with a few exceptions.

Some churches use sermon-based groups, which is genius from an educational point of view, and the normal course of sermon-based groups is steady. These churches don't face all of the ups and downs of alignment series. While there's a push to join groups every semester, it's not the bandwagon effect over and over and over again. The bandwagon is fatiguing, which leads to the second point.

If the church has used alignment series for more than three years, it will experience a diminishing return. For years now, I've told the story of a church that had dramatic success in connecting all of its people into groups within a nine-month three-campaign push. The pastor was engaged. They were naturals at creating their own curriculum. They launched multiple campaigns year after year. Then they began facing a steady skid downward. When I caught up with them, groups were at an all-time low. Did the campaigns fail?

Their campaigns succeeded for the first two years. But by the third year, campaign fatigue had set in. They were excellent at the sprint of the campaign, but they suffered when the sprint became a marathon. Most churches will suffer this too. Once the majority of the congregation is connected into groups and the church has run alignment series for two or three years, it's time for a change. If they don't make the switch, groups will decline, except for two scenarios.

When is a church beyond alignment series? Before anyone starts demonizing campaigns, first consider some solid reasons to launch an alignment series. The church's progress will determine whether you need an alignment series or not.

Why Churches Need Alignment Series

First, if the church is rapidly growing, it will constantly need alignments just to keep up. While the weekend service is a great attractor, groups are the place where people are connected and discipled. Alignment series are the best way to recruit new leaders and get a lot of people connected into groups very quickly. If the church is growing, then keep alignments going.

Second, if the congregation faces continual turnover, then alignment series are necessary. Churches near a military base, or in a college town, or full of young people, see a steady turnover. Their members are regularly deployed, graduating, or getting married and moving to the suburbs.

Manna Church in Fayetteville, North Carolina, sits next to Fort Bragg. They regularly lose a thousand people every year who are either deployed or reassigned. Alignment series have helped them connect the regular influx of new members. Manna "deployed" their groups all over the world, and then they got smart and started campuses near military bases across the United States. Different bases, but the same church!

Rapid growth and steady turnover are fertile environments for alignment series. Every year the church will need new groups. In order to have new groups, more new leaders are required. After all, the primary purpose of alignment series is leader recruitment. Since most people don't see themselves as leaders, a six-week alignment series gives them the opportunity to test-drive a group and show them that they are the leaders they never knew they were.

When to Start Using Alignment Series

Through my book, courses, and coaching groups, pastors learn how to launch and maximize alignment series. These are churches that have never done alignment series or have just started. After many years of alignments, they know more about how to keep groups going once the six weeks is over. Churches must begin with the end in mind. In fact, I encourage pastors to develop their coaching structure before they recruit a single leader or start a group. That's one key to lasting groups.

If the church has a wide gap between its weekly attendance and its group participation, then the church needs an alignment series to catch up. Now, if there are other Bible study options available at the church, don't count them in "unconnected" category. These classes or studies provide the connection people need. Those who are committed to Sunday school, midweek Bible studies, or other Bible studies don't need to join a small group. That is their small group. The concern should be for those who attend only the weekend service and are not connected otherwise.

Once most of people have joined groups, the church can certainly use alignment series with relevant topics to reach its community. Alignment series can be used occasionally to launch a new initiative in the church or just reinvigorate the church's groups. But their continual use will eventually produce a diminishing return.

▶ *Case Study* ◀

LifeBridge Christian Church

LifeBridge Christian Church is a 125-year-old church in Longmont, Colorado (Denver suburb). Over the past twenty-five years with Senior Pastor Rick Rusaw, what was originally First Christian Church of Longmont became one of the most innovative churches in the country. They were innovators in both the *Externally Focused Church* movement and *The Neighboring Church*.[15] As early adopters, LifeBridge has done alignment series for a very long time. In fact, they had done campaigns to the point that they made an alarming discovery.

"LifeBridge has tried a lot of different models over the years and has experienced a lot of success," said Sean Badeer, small group pastor. "Our approach with groups for a long time was to make a splash. In six weeks we would recruit group hosts, sign up a bunch of new group members in the lobby, and thrive for six weeks. After that, the groups would usually disband until the next campaign. In our next to last series, we recruited leaders, and then we gave our congregation a little sushi-like menu to choose a group. We pieced these groups together with sign-ups. We just saw minimal success. Very few people stuck around after the series ended. We ended up with a lot of discouraged leaders. In our last series, Rick asked for leaders in the service. He challenged them to fill out a card. I think we got two cards. It was pretty clear to all of us that the way we were doing things was done."

Without disrupting the groups that continued to meet, LifeBridge introduced a new groups strategy that upped the ante on commitment and discipleship. "We went to the polar opposite of short-term and plug and play. We went with *Rooted*," Badeer said. In *Rooted*, group members were required to pay for their curriculum, which was a first, meet for ten weeks rather than five or six weeks, and complete five days of daily homework each week before the group meeting. "We were not choosing a topical study that felt like anybody could be a part of it. It was explicitly religious. But it would challenge our people to grow closer to God, to others, and to their purpose. The whole thing felt very different to what we were doing before."

While not being averse to trying new things, LifeBridge had never offered anything like this before. They started with two rounds of pilot groups. In the first pilot, about forty people (mostly staff) went through the *Rooted* material. Facilitators came out of the first pilot for the second pilot, which involved about a hundred of the church's key volunteers. In the initial launch to the whole church, around three hundred people participated in *Rooted* groups. Now, three years later, LifeBridge has seen over twelve hundred people go through *Rooted*.

"These groups have continued in community. People have come back and facilitated new groups for others," Badeer shared. Not only has *Rooted* helped to deepen the spiritual walk of LifeBridge's congregation, it has also served to produce an abundance of new group leaders. "*Rooted* has become a significant leadership pipeline for us. We ask every facilitator to bring a future facilitator to the final training of the ten-week *Rooted* experience. We would see people who we would never have found ourselves. There is something about being tapped on the shoulder by their leader and hearing, 'I see something in you that I think God is going to use.'"

In one instance, a *Rooted* participant—who was baptized at the celebration event at the end of the ten-week study—decided to lead a group of his own the next time around. "He didn't feel qualified. He did what he needed to do in leading the group. Then, he got to baptize somebody in his *Rooted* group, which is just amazing to me. That's the picture of discipleship: when you see people taking on this mission that they've experienced themselves, and then turn around and give it to others.

Is It Time for the Church to Move beyond Alignment Series?

Alignment series are great sprints toward connecting a lot of people in a hurry. But disciple-making is a marathon, not a sprint. The ultimate goal of groups is to make disciples. Disciples are not the end result of a process. Disciples are crafted. Eventually, the church will want video-based-curriculum-dependent newbies to be able to rightly divide the Word of Truth and facilitate a discussion leading toward on-going life change. You can't grow disciples in fits and starts. As Eugene Peterson once titled a book, it's *A Long Obedience in the Same Direction*.

Alignment series can help you or hurt you. Just like hot sauce, you've got to know how much to use and when. Otherwise, you'll numb your taste buds for alignments. Is it time to start an alignment series? Or is it time to stop?

In Jesus' work with his disciples, there are three distinct phases: "Come and follow" (Matthew 4:19), "Come and die" (Luke 9:23), and "Go and make" (Matthew 28:18–20). While some churches attempt to start "serious" discipleship groups with "Come and Die," it's much easier to start groups with "Come and Follow," and then lead them into maturity to reach "Come and Die."

The purpose of the "Come and Follow" stage is connection. Whether the church is trying to connect their worship attendance, the neighborhood, or both, this connection purpose can largely be achieved by offering a felt-needs topic with an alignment series, as described in *Exponential Groups*. This low commitment, short-term approach allows potential leaders and their groups to test drive a group and begin the habit of meeting together. While the primary purpose is connection, other purposes—including leadership development and spiritual growth—can certainly take place at the "Come and follow" stage.

The danger in "connection groups" is in seeing them as an end in themselves. Rather, they should be viewed as the starting point for discipleship that will gradually increase the maturity of the group members and group leaders. Some pastors embrace the notion that things must be kept easy and ask for a low commitment in order to produce maximum results. After working with churches in their alignment series for nearly twenty years now, I've found that the reality is the low-commitment and low-requirement approaches eventually produce low maturity. What's worse is that as the church continues into a minority Christian culture, the lack of challenge is off-putting to those who seek depth and genuine relationship with God and others. In the twenty-first century, people are looking for answers. They desire a cause to live for. Once they are engaged in groups, they need more. They need the challenge to "Come and die."

The purpose of the "Come and Die" phase is growth and spiritual maturity. Please don't read those words as "deeper" teaching and more Bible facts. While the intellect is important—after all, God gave humans a book and a brain—there is so much more to discipling the whole person. This is more than an academic exercise. A well-rounded approach to discipleship must take into consideration every aspect of a person's life and being—physical, emotional, relational, financial, intellectual, and other areas. (As this topic is too large to explore here, I have a future book in the works.)

The mission of the church in making disciples is to baptize them and teach them to obey what Jesus commanded. Obedience and surrender are best evidenced in a person's attitude and actions. Rather than using all of the clichés about "walking your talk" and so forth, the point is the end result of discipleship is someone who more closely resembles Jesus Christ. They are dying to themselves, and their ways of dealing with things are being replaced with those of Jesus. The self is sacrificed to produce genuine transformation.

The church can turn up the temperature on discipleship in their groups through the curriculum and leadership training offered. Again, this is not an invitation to teach groups to parse Greek verbs. Curriculum should be a balance of personal time with God, a group discussion of the Bible, assignments to turn words into action, and accountability to check progress.

Curriculum is not just a course of study, but also an action plan for integrating the teaching of the Bible into daily life. More than an assent to a belief statement, it should help believers live and breathe Scripture in their daily lives. There are excellent study formats that can help turn up the temperature of discipleship: *Rooted* (experiencerooted.com), *The Neighboring Life: Getting Better at What Jesus Says Matters Most* by Rick Rusaw and Brian Mavis (Nashville: Nelson, 2016), *Emotionally Healthy Relationships Workbook: Discipleship That Deeply Changes Your Relationship with Others* by Pete Scazzero (Grand Rapids: Zondervan, 2017), *D-Life Journal* by Dr. Bill Wilks and Dr. John Herring (Life Bible Study, 2017), or *Growing Up: How to Be a Disciple Who Makes Disciples* by Robby Gallaty (Nashville: B&H Books, 2013). Even a format like the Discovery Bible Study Method, which uses the same nine questions for every passage of Scripture, helps group members to apply God's word and live it out. The expectation is that the power of God residing in every believer (Ephesians 1:18–20), accompanied by studying the Bible and helping them interact with other believers, will produce transformed lives.

A few years ago, I was working with a small group director who had moved to the United States. In his country of origin, there was a high expectation of believers learning, doing, and sharing what they've learned from the very beginning of their relationship with God. He was a little beside himself when he came to the US and discovered that many believers learned biblical truth without much intention of practicing what they learned or sharing it with others. When he challenged people in his church to high commitment approaches to discipleship, he found resistance. I asked him if he had ever heard the analogy of the frog and the kettle. He had not.

I explained this common story about how placing frogs in hot water caused them to jump out. Yet by placing frogs in cold water and then gradually turning up the temperature, the frogs remained in the hot water because the change was gradual. I told him he was putting his disciples in hot water and that's why they were resisting. (If you're shaking your head at this point about the reverse implications of this analogy, I apologize. I'll switch gears before this turns into martyrdom, which is no joking matter.)

For average American church members, the move from the worship service to a group is a pretty big step. If the benefit of a group is unproven, then they need an opportunity to try out this environment in a short-term, low-commitment way. An alignment series fits the bill. If they've had a positive experience, then the group may agree to continue into a follow-up series. Once these two studies have been completed, then it's more likely the group will continue.

Group leaders are given a leadership pathway (as discussed in chapter 9). Group members should also be given a curriculum pathway. This could be based on the results of the group's health assessment (chapter 11). Curriculum should also lead the group into new experiences and even into taking risks as a group. These risks could include things like the three-hour prayer experience in *Rooted*, the neighborhood map in *The Neighboring Life*, or the genogram in *Emotionally-Healthy Spirituality*. The goal of these exercises is to learn to trust God in deeper ways, to hear God, and to learn about oneself.

Curriculum for the sake of curriculum is worthless. Checking off a list of studies doesn't guarantee growth. But using curriculum as a vehicle to produce growth and lasting change is worthwhile. What is your curriculum producing? What are your groups producing? Using an assessment from chapter 11 of this workbook, evaluate the progress your people, your groups, and your church is making.

The third phase from Scripture is "Go and Make." While these phases don't need to occur in sequential order, the goal is to make disciples who make disciples. After all, that's how a church knows it's making disciples. If the people in the church are not making disciples, then they are not disciples. The appropriate term for them would be "the crowd." In the Gospels, Jesus spent 73 percent of his time with his disciples.[16] He didn't devote vast amounts of time to serving the crowd.

"Go and Make" implies that church members are thinking about others more than about themselves and their own needs. They become self-feeders. The focus is on servant leadership at various levels. While most people in the church will not have the title of leader, they will have influence over people around them. The goal is to multiply their lives and their abilities. Jesus spent three and a half years investing in twelve disciples, who after his departure developed others and took the message of the gospel throughout their known world, establishing churches, and making disciples.

This is the place where pastors equip the church to do the work of the ministry (Ephesians 4:11–12). Over the past thirty years, the church has catered to people in order to serve a Christian consumer culture. As a result, a growing gap has emerged between staff and volunteers, or clergy and laity as it was once known. People are asked to volunteer to serve the church and the efforts of the church staff. But the volunteers are the church!

Members should be challenged to pursue and develop their gifts. Resources like *Network* by Bruce Bugbee (Zondervan, 2005) and *Leadershift* by Don Cousins and Bruce Bugbee (David C. Cook, 2008) create the philosophical foundation for gifts-based ministry that is truly satisfying to church members and effective in reaching the neighborhood. After all, ministry is not something pastors do to people. Ministry is the purpose of the church body, not the leaders of the institution. People need to serve in meaningful ways in order to grow spiritually. Meaningless volunteer roles cannot meet this purpose.

Since a church of any size cannot assess and recognize the gifts of every church member, groups play an essential role in helping people discover, develop, and use their gifts. This is more than another assessment. There is an expectation for people to take responsibility for understanding and implementing their gifts to fulfill the mission of the church. There is also a responsibility for the church to release not just ministry responsibilities, but also the authority to carry them out.

One more step lies beyond identifying and using gifts: members developing other members. Every person in every role in the church—including members, pastors, and church staff—must multiply what they are doing in the lives of others. This is one of the primary purposes of groups: leadership development. The church must embrace hero-making as articulated by Dave Ferguson and Dr. Warren Bird. The pastor is not the hero in the church. The staff members are not the heroes. The members are not the heroes. But they are all called to make heroes. They are all called to invest in others and help them flourish in ministry. They are called to work themselves out of a job so that a new ministry, group, or church can be launched to serve others and repeat the process.

These three phases may not be the only phases, and they don't necessarily need to be taken in this exact order (or else some churches will camp on phase two until Jesus returns and never get to Phase 3!). The point is that everyone must be challenged to take a next step at every phase. Those who attend only the worship service must be challenged to join a group. Everyone in a group must be challenged to take what they learn to heart and mature in their faith as evidenced by their actions and attitudes. Those who are maturing must reach out to their neighborhoods and share their hope. Those who are serving must develop others to serve.

Attractional services and advertising built some great churches in between the 1980s and 2000s. The next thirty years, however, will be much different than the last thirty. This statement is not meant to discount what happened over these decades, but it's time to gear up for what is next. In working with churches across North America, I've visited many formerly great churches. At one point in time, the church was the shining beacon in the community. Maybe they were the first church to offer contemporary worship music and relevant messages. People came in droves, until every other church in town followed the model. Now those churches are dwindling. They are formerly great. There is a shift that must take place in order to engage people in the twenty-first century. These concluding thoughts reveal part of the thinking needed for the church to flourish in an increasingly minority Christian culture.

Where Is Your Church?

As you consider your congregation, where do you believe your members and attendees are in terms of their spiritual growth and development? How are they connected? What phase of spiritual growth are they in? In this final exercise in this workbook, take some time to evaluate what your church has produced in your members so far. Then you will know what next steps to offer in order to further the growth of your groups and members.

In the chart below, fill in the number of groups and ministries contributing to each phase, and then add the number of members in each phase.

Worship Attendance Only

This number represents people who attend only worship and are not connected in the life of the church in any other way. This includes everyone who attends at least once per year.

Phase 1: Come and Follow

This is the number of people who are involved in short-term, low-commitment groups and ministries. This would include groups formed for alignment series, semester-based groups and classes, entry-level serving opportunities, and other short-term experiences designed to connect people together.

Phase 2: Come and Die

This is the number of people involved in on-going small groups (in their second semester together and beyond), as well as on-going classes and ministries where life change is demonstrated through assessment and accountability.

Phase 3: Go and Make

This is the number represents the disciples making disciples and leaders developing new leaders. True hero-making is taking place.

The exercise is for the purpose of understanding, in general, what should be offered next in your church. An assessment to evaluate each member could also be developed.

Phase	Worship Attendance Only	Phase 1: Come and Follow	Phase 2: Come and Die	Phase 3: Go and Make
Groups & Ministries				
Members				

If the majority of the church's members and attendees fall in the Worship Attendance column, then the church should consider a short-term, low-commitment alignment series or church-wide campaign to identify potential leaders and form groups.

If the majority of the church is in Phase 1, then discipleship methods such as *Rooted*, *The Neighboring Life*, *D-Life*, *D-Groups*, *Emotionally-Healthy Spirituality*, the *Discovery Bible Study Method*, 3DM Ministries, Real Life Ministries, or similar should be considered to raise the bar on leadership and discipleship in the church.

If the majority of the church is in Phase 2, then emphasis should be given to multiplication by every member multiplying their life in another member, every leader developing a leader, every staff member developing an apprentice, and every pastor developing a pastor. Concepts like *Leadershift* and *Hero-Maker* should be employed at every level.

God wants to work in your church. How much are you willing to get out of the way to allow him to work? How much are you willing to learn in order to lead better? How much are you willing to risk in order to receive a better return? How much are you willing to change from what has always worked? Are you prepared for exponential groups and exponential growth? This is what is now required.

APPENDIX

Sample Sermons for Promoting Groups and Recruiting Leaders

"Community in Christ"
Sermon by Pastor Don Wink
Lutheran Church of the Atonement, Barrington, Illinois[17]

This is week three of three in a short series called "Growing through Change." Today we're focusing on community and on that which we hold in common—our life together. I promise I'm not going to embarrass you or ask you to show this to anybody else, but it'll help in this next bit. Grab a piece of paper or something to write on and then draw a box of any size. It doesn't need to be good. There are no grades, and everyone gets a participation trophy. In the lower left-hand corner of the box, write a word or a symbol or something. Write an abbreviation for chocolate. In the lower left-hand corner write "chocolate," and in the lower right-hand corner write "vanilla." Now this is the most complicated thing I'm going to ask you to do: Somewhere on that continuum from left to right, mark your ice cream preference of chocolate versus vanilla with an "x." I recognize some of you might not like either, but this is just part of the grand experiment we're doing here together.

Does everyone have an "x" somewhere on there? My guess is that if we had the ability to plot all your various marks into one graph, we'd see a range and a bit of a scattergram across the spectrum from chocolate to vanilla. I thought for a long, long time that vanilla was the most popular flavor by a huge factor. But then I saw recently that chocolate is gaining on it. So here's the thing: When we are in a community and both chocolate and vanilla are offered freely, there's no tension within the community. Everyone can have what they want. It's when change starts to happen that it gets more complicated.

I was working with a coach one time who said that in any change, the three most important questions are: What does this mean to me? What does this mean to me? and What does this mean to me? So what if we were to say, "I know that we've always freely offered chocolate and vanilla, but the latest health research indicates that the antioxidant properties of chocolate are so compelling, we're going to offer more chocolate than vanilla. For those of you who are toward the left side of things there, you're going to be happy about that. For those who are more toward the vanilla side of things might be saying, "Hmm, not so sure I liked that." What if the second wave of change involved receiving a volume discount if we buy chocolate exclusively? Then we would say, "And since not that many people are into vanilla anyway, we're just going to do chocolate 100 percent of the time." How do you feel about that now? Maybe not so great. Maybe you start to think that this isn't really your box anymore. This isn't really your community. There's not a place for you here. You might go find another box that offers vanilla.

So why am I using this illustration? I'm using it because I'm trying to find something with a range of preferences that isn't too volatile. The Cubs and Sox are playing this weekend, so I know I can't talk about that. But in any community, regardless of what the issue is, regardless of what the dimensions are, regardless of what the polls are, there is going to be a range of responses. And as change starts to rattle us a little bit, we might have some strong responses.

Here's something I learned recently. It turns out that when there are two polls in which people are operating, we tend to exaggerate our impressions of what other people believe in a poll that's different from ours. We think that they believe more strongly than they really do. So whatever you think about the other poll, if you were to ask them that same question, you would not see it in the same measure. And here's where it gets really interesting. The researchers found that the more educated a person was and the more involved they were in the political process, the more that was true. So a lot of times I would be inclined to think that folks just don't know. But it turns out that the more you know, the more deeply entrenched you become. The more involved you are, the more deeply entrenched you become. And if you watch television, you will overestimate the response of the other by a factor of three. So what happens? By its nature, community is wide and broad and deep and diverse. It has a wide range of expressions and possibilities. But sometimes when change happens, community has a way of shrinking in on itself, which can then repeat and repeat and repeat until we end up with our small tribes of likeminded people.

Jesus has a better way. In fact, his way is so important to him that he prays it on the last night of his life. He prays that the community be so compelling that all who follow him—all who carry his name, all who profess him as Lord—would be one. I don't think he means that we should all think the same. I think he means that we shouldn't let what we think divide us. His measure of oneness is pretty strong. He says that the same kind of unity that there is between him and his Father is the same kind of unity that he expects and makes possible among us. That's strong.

While the language Jesus uses is a little vague, the apostle Paul has the same idea but uses more concrete language. So I want to spend some time there. In his letter to the church in Colossae, Paul says that this is what community looks like, that these are the behaviors of those in community with one another. He lists five things right up front: compassion, kindness, humility, meekness, and patience. Probably the only word in there that requires definition is *meekness*. It's misunderstood because it rhymes with weakness, but it's actually the opposite of that. It is restrained strength. Some Bibles translate it as "gentleness." I don't know that they really get that strength dimension.

So we see these words—*compassion*, *kindness*, *humility*, *meekness*, and *patience*—and we say, well, these are good things. Why wouldn't we want them? But we say those are good things, because we've been so influenced by Christianity and by Jesus in particular. When Paul wrote those words, those were seen as detriments in the Roman Empire, character faults. Compassion? That's for wimps. Kindness? Forget about it. Humility? No, it's all about me. Meekness? No, show your strength; make them fear you. Patience? Come on, I want it yesterday. These attributes are building of community within the church, even at the same time as they're seen as detrimental to the individual enrollment society.

What is it that stands in the way of community? Paul talks about that as well. It's kind of a standard list and things that you might expect: anger, wrath, malice, slander, and abusive or filthy language. These things are damaging to community. Whatever might divide you, Paul said—whether you're a certain gender or nationality or your economic status, your liberty or lack thereof—nothing matters more than what you have together in Christ.

I asked the question this week to the great source Google: What is it that damages human community? The first three results were most interesting, especially since they disagreed with one another. One said that humans destroy human community. The second one blamed technology. The third said that it's inevitable: When you put people together, something eventually will be destructive. Clearly it can be any or all of those things; they don't have to be an agreement.

Then I thought about my experience as a pastor. What have I found damaging to Christian community over time? I landed on these three answers, though you might have others. The first one is demands. Demands are damaging of community. You can think of demands as being preferences that are taken too far.

We're celebrating our nation's independence this week—which means we're celebrating both freedom and democracy, right? But freedom within democracy by necessity gets restrained somewhat. Individual freedom is restrained within democracy in order for us to be able to live together in a way that works. In our nation, we have a true democracy where it's one person, one vote. We also have a representative democracy, where people are elected or appointed to fulfill functions and make decisions. Interestingly, it works the same way in the church. At least in our church, we have some decisions that are one person, one vote, and we have other decisions that are delegated to called and elected and appointed leaders. Demands become damaging, however, when through the process of either direct democracy or delegated decision making someone says, "I can't live with that. I insist on it being this way. And in fact, if I don't get my way, I'm going to leave. Or if I don't get my way, I'm going to behave in such a way that you wished I had left!" This type of demand undermines and damages our community we.

The second is pretty much the opposite of demands: indifference. Now, sometimes indifference toward an outcome can actually be a good thing in community. That is, when everyone is happy with whatever we decide together. But it's actually damaging if someone has indifference toward the people who are involved or toward being part of the community. When they say, "I can take it or leave it." In this, there's no cohesiveness, no coherence.

The third one is grudges or resentments. These bind us to the past. There's no movement when we're stuck in grudges. The apostle Paul talks a lot about this. He understands and says that if you have a grievance, bear with one another. It's inevitable that when you put two people together for long enough, they will have points of difference and disagreement. If they expand on this, then it becomes true exponentially. And so Paul talks also about forgiveness, about letting go.

But another problem here is that we can have some misunderstandings or misconceptions about forgiveness. We think that if we forgive someone that they're getting away with it. But if we're insistent on holding a grudge against someone, we're forcing them to pay over and over and over again for something that's now in the past. And it's possible they're not even thinking about it anymore. In this case, who's paying the cost of holding this grudge? We are. So we need to let it go. The beauty of forgiveness is that it does not require cooperation or confession on the part of the other. We do not need to wait to forgive someone until they say they're sorry. What if the person you need to forgive is no longer living or has moved away or is unwilling to participate in the healing process? Forgiveness can happen without the cooperation or confession from the other person. But even if that person does choose to cooperate and confess, we still may hold that grudge—which only keeps us stuck in the past.

If these are three things that can damage community, what are the antidotes? Let's take the human body as an example. The healthy human body has pathogens within it, but not everyone who has pathogens is going to become sick. Some people have a quality immune system. So we need to ask ourselves how we as a body can strengthen our immune response, especially when we're facing demands, indifference, and grudges. Paul has some things to say about that too. Expanding on what I already mentioned about forgiveness, Paul adds love, peace, and thanksgiving. I'm going to put them in the order I think of least difficult to do to most difficult to do, which is thanksgiving, love, and peace.

When we're thankful, there are a lot of negative things that just can't happen and resentments become smaller. So my invitation to you, if you finding yourself fighting any of these community-damaging attributes, is to start with thanksgiving. Write down a list of what you're thankful for. Give yourself a period of time of perhaps three or five minutes. We challenged one of our children to do this when she was in an anxious preteen phase in sixth grade and gratitude was very far from her experience. I remember being exasperated and saying, "Natalie, you are not thankful about anything." She said nothing, but she went into the other room and came back a half hour later with a two-sided list of what she was thankful for. But my guess is that her heart was in a different place after she did this. You don't need to fill up two sides of paper, but please take up the challenge.

The second immune building response is love. Love in the Bible is rarely an emotion. It's more of an action. In particular, the kind of action where we empty ourselves and make room for another, especially someone who's difficult. The model for this is Jesus's self-emptying on the cross. There's no greater love than this: that one lay down their life for their friends. The third one is peace. Peace is not the absence of conflict, but the restoration to health and vitality and well-being of those around us. Where do we see brokenness, and how might we participate in peacemaking?

What does a healthy, vibrant, life-giving community look like? I had the great gift and pleasure of being with a number of families last weekend for the wedding of two kids who grew up at our church. Weddings are always celebratory, but the added quality was that this was a celebration of the faith community that helped form these two now-grown people. They became close here at church, and so many of the people who had been formative in their lives were present at that wedding, celebrating with them. But it wasn't just about the couple. As I looked around the room at those in attendance, I knew their stories. There was a death in one family this year. Someone else retired. This person lost their job. There's extended family illness. There's estrangement. There are unresolved issues, and on and on and on. But we were there as one in Christ, celebrating the life that had happened here and that would continue to happen here.

There are other expressions of vibrant community besides weddings. This week, we're doing Vacation Bible School here. It's going to be raucous. It's going to be wild. It's going to be crazy. Some of the leaders are going to say, "Why do I do this?" Well, you do this because kids like these are being formed—just like the ones who married each other last weekend. And when we're done doing VBS here, we're going to take some of our volunteers to another church and offer that kind of gift to the wider community, so that they can also experience vibrant Christian community.

Do you want this for yourselves? I certainly want this for you. But even more than you wanting it and even more than me wanting it for you, Jesus wants it for you and Jesus gives it to you. Thanks be to God. Amen.

"The Connection Commandment"
Sermon by Dr. Tony Evans
Oak Cliff Bible Fellowship, Dallas, Texas[18]

Opening Prayer: Worshiping here today in our weakness with our limitations, with our frailty, with our failures, we still come and we still want to hear from Heaven. Please let Heaven scream in our ears today, and may our ears be open and not clogged. We're going to give you the glory in Jesus' name. Amen.

Please stand for the reading of the Scripture today. Open your Bible to Matthew 22, beginning with verse 34:

> But when the Pharisees heard that Jesus had silent the Sadducees, they gathered themselves together. One of them a lawyer asked him a question testing him. Teacher, which is the great commandment in the law? He said to him, "You shall love the Lord, your God, with all of your heart, with all of your soul, and with all of your mind. This is the great and foremost commandment. The second is like it. You shall love your neighbor as yourself. On these two commandments depend the whole law and the prophet."

And all God's people said amen.

A young man one day was seeking to get a job with a foresting crew who was chopping down trees, and he was pretty good at it. He went to the captain of the crew and said, "I'd like you to hire me because I think I could do a good job for you chopping down trees." He said, "Well, let me see you work, because this is hard work and I really need to know you know how to do this." The young man went out and took his axe and he put on a show for the captain of the crew, the foreman, as he felled the tree lickety-split. The foreman said, "You're hired. Right now you're hired. I'm impressed with what you did."

The problem came a week later after the young man had been hired. The foreman called him into his office and said, "I'm sorry, son, to let you know we're going to have to let you go. We're going to have to release you. I was impressed with you when you came here, but every day your work has slowed up. The amount of trees has lessened that you chop down. In fact, on the day you came, you were the best; one week later, you're one of the worst. I'm going to have to let you go. Pick up your final check. I'm sorry it didn't work out."

The young man said to him, "I don't understand. I've worked like a dog every day. In fact, I've skipped my lunch breaks. I've skipped the coffee breaks. I've been here overtime, and I don't know how having worked so hard I've achieved so little when I started so well."

The foreman looked at him and, knowing he was sincere that he really did work hard even though he was declining in his effectiveness, he said, "Son, let me ask you a question. During this week of chopping down the trees, did you ever stop to sharpen your axe?"

He says, "I've been too busy working to sharpen my axe. I've been too busy trying to chop down trees to sharpen my axe."

The foreman says, "That's your problem. No matter how hard you work, if the axe is not sharp it won't achieve the goal the work is designed to produce. Son, you failed not because you didn't work hard, but because you were working hard with a dull tool."

For many of us, it's not because we're not trying hard. It's that what we're trying we're using a dull instrument that has yet to be sharpened, and as a result the work doesn't seem to be paying off. This morning I would like to sharpen your tool, my tool, our tool, so that what we do is accomplishing what it's designed to accomplish.

In verses 35 and 36, a lawyer, one of the Pharisees, came to Jesus and he asked Jesus a question: "Teacher, which is the great commandment in the law?" Let's look at the question a little bit first. There were Ten Commandments; we all know that, the Ten Commandments. These Ten Commandments had 613 what are called statutes and ordinances; that is the application of the Ten Commandments in the various circumstances of life that was to govern Israel. There were Ten Commandments, and then there were 613 statute and ordinances. Now the 613 statutes and ordinances were divided into two categories, one being positive (248), and the other being negative (365), making the 613 that were to reflect the ten. They wanted to know we're trying to keep up with all that God wants us to do—Ten Commandments and 613 statutes and ordinances. But so that we get our priorities straight, which is number one?

Of all the things God expects of us, what is number one? Perhaps you come to church every week and you hear a sermon about this, a sermon about that, and I'm supposed to do this and I'm supposed to do that, God expects this, and God expects that, and sometimes they seem a little overwhelming, and perhaps, you want to know like the lawyer: God just give me one thing. Just tell me which one I need to do to be straight, so that I'm well on my way to what I'm supposed to be as a Christian. Give me the big dog, not the little puppy. Give me that thing that if I grab that I got it. That's what the lawyer says, "Give me the commandment that is foremost of all."

Jesus answered his question by quoting Deuteronomy 6:4–5. In the Hebrew it's called the *Shema*; it means to hear. "You shall love," he says in verse 37. "You shall love the Lord your God with all your heart, with all your soul, with all your mind." He tells him that the greatest commandment, the thing that overshadows everything else, has to do with relationship, not with rules, because it's got to do with love. Since I know you're not asking "What's love got to do with it?" Jesus says that the thing that is to mark you and me is the thing called love. It would be the centerpiece of everything else God says; all Ten Commandments and all 613 statutes and ordinances ought to be reduced to this thing called love.

We've defined love on a number of occasions, but let me define love again. Please notice that love must be more than a feeling, because you can command it. He says, "What is the greatest commandment?" Whatever love is, it's commandable, which means it must transcend emotions because you can't always command your emotions. Biblical love is the decision to passionately and righteously seek the well-being of another. It is a decision. Biblical love starts with a decision, whether or not there is an accompanying emotion. Sometime the emotion will be there; sometimes the emotion won't be there. That has nothing to do whether love is there, because love is a decision of the will whether or not it is accompanied by a feeling in the emotion, because it's commandable. You can decide to do it or not do it.

He says that the thing that ought to mark the greatest thing of all is love, and then he says it is love of God. More than anything else, God wants you to love him. He wants a relationship with you and me. Without love, nothing else matters. First Corinthians 13 says, "If you have not love, whatever else you do becomes noise." If you're here today but you don't love him, you just came to an event. He says the greatest commandment of all—stay with me here—is that you should love the Lord your God. How am I to love him? "With all your heart, all your soul, all your mind." Mark 12 has another one: "and with all your strength."

Now, last time I checked if you got my heart, my mind, my soul, and my body, I don't have anything else. You own me. How much does God want you to love him? He tells you. He says, "With all." He wants it all. He wants everything that makes you *you* to be in love with him. He doesn't just want you to come to church. He doesn't just want you to pray a prayer a day to keep the devil away. He doesn't just want you to read a verse. He wants you to love him.

He says, "I want you to love me with all of your heart." That is the core of your being. That is the pump that breathes life into every other part of you. "From the deepest part of your being, I want you to love me." He says that when it comes to what you think, how you're thinking, when it comes to your mind, "I want your brain to love me. When it comes to your soul—that is your personality and your self-consciousness—whenever you are awake I want your awakeness to be in love with me." He says, "I want you to love me with your body. That is, with your fingers and your toes and your eyes and your hands and your legs and every part of your frame. I want you to love me, and I want you to love me with all of it." In other words, "if you love me with all of it, there is nothing else to love because I have it all." To put it another way, "Anything else you do love has to fit in with your love with me, because you just gave me all of it."

As I meditated on this Scripture a week ago, it dawned on me: Here it is, this is our problem, this explains it all for all of us. He says, "Love me with all," and most of us love him with some. It's not that we don't love him with all. He can have some of my heart. He can have some of my mind. He can have some of my soul. He can have some of my strength. But you're talking about *all*. You're talking about this all-consuming love that God is demanding, requiring, and requesting to receive. That's why the Scripture says, "When we share our love with him with the world, we lose our love relationship with him."

First John 2:15–17 says, "If you love the world or the things that are in the world, the love of the Father is not in you." Because in antithesis to the love of God is the love of the world. The world is that system headed by Satan that leaves God out. When God is no longer part of the equation that's called worldliness; when you love something that excludes him, this means that God must recoil because he will not share a love relationship. What is missing today? The reason why we are so distant from God is we love him with some and he demands to be loved with all. All your mind, all your heart, all your strength, all your soul, all of your heart. He wants it all. We are to give God comprehensive love commitment.

I saw a car some months ago pull into our parking lot with a rabbit foot dangling from the rearview mirror. I'm sure it was a car of a visitor, because I just can't conceive a member of the Oak Cliff Bible Fellowship, who's been here for any extended period of time, having a rabbit foot dangling from the mirror, so I'm sure it was a visitor. A rabbit that can't even keep its own foot shouldn't be looked to to take care of you! But it is amazing the things that people who name the name of Jesus Christ, who claim to know God, gravitate to because they're not all that convinced that he is enough and that his methods are enough.

What we do is we share a love that God is unwilling to share. What a lot of people want is to date God, but he's looking for a ring. We want to date him. We want to have a good time with him. We want to hang out with him. We don't want to live with him. We don't want this marriage thing. We don't want this full attachment. What we do often—permitting many exceptions to this for many, maybe even most—is we camouflage our love for God with religion, because if I can look like I love him, I can look like it. If I can say the right Christianese, if I could say the right words, if I can hang out in the right church, if I can carry my Bible under my arm, if I can wave my hand and wave it in the air, wave it like I just don't care, if I can shout and jump and celebrate—if I can do all that, then I can at least give the impression to others, and maybe even trick me, into thinking I love God.

Like the time I foolishly picked up an apple only to discover it was wax as I bit into it. It looked real. It looked so real. Like that embarrassing moment that I had when I met a sister in church who I hadn't seen in a long time and asked her, "How long have you been pregnant? How far along are you?" She said,

"I ain't pregnant." She looked pregnant to me. How embarrassing, but I got an impression that wasn't correct. Before we finish today I want you to remove the facade. I can fool you; you can fool me; none us can fool him. He says, "I want you to love me so much, there's nothing else left for anything or anyone who doesn't come in on that love cycle, who's not attached to love that love train."

Now, we just said to love God with all of it—not many of it, some of it, much of it, most of it—but to say, "Okay, everything that I am," because those four things make up all that you are. "Everything I am is assigned to loving you." The question is, how do you know if you're loving him? If it's more than a feeling—and sometimes I feel it, sometimes I don't, sometimes I have goose bumps, sometimes I don't—how do I know if I'm loving him and not just saying I'm loving him, and that I really love him with everything I've got?

Let me read to you from First John 5. Here's what John says in the second half of verse 2, "We know we love God when we observe his commandments." Verse 3, "For this is the love of God, that we keep his commandments, and his commandments are not burdensome." You love God when you act consistent to his expectations, requirements, and demands. You don't love God just because you're feeling it right now. It could be that you're feeling it because you love him, but you can feel it and not love him. He says, "The way you know you love me is that you are thinking to align your decisions with my expectations of my commandments."

Let me help you from a negative way to know whether you love God or not. How bad do you feel when you disappoint him? If I love him, I want to seek his well-being—that is, seek his glory, seek his name advancement, seek him being highlighted in my life through conforming my actions to his expectations. The way I know that I love him is how bad I feel when I fail him. My goal is not to fail him; my goal is to please him. If you want to fall in love with him—that is, if you want to love him with all you got—you need to begin to make your decisions to align your heart, your mind, your strength, and your soul to his commandments; then you have begun the process of going in your love for him. If there is not that decision, there is not that love no matter how much you enjoy church.

Let's put it this way. Let's say you have a trainer. You go to this trainer, this man or woman, once a week to train you, to lift weights, to exercise, and to guide you in the transformation you want in your life. You want to look different; you want to feel different; you want to lose weight, or whatever you want to do. Once a week, you go to your trainer. Let's say your trainer and you have a meeting once a week for two hours and it's every Sunday. Every Sunday, you and your trainer meet at the local gym because every Sunday you want your trainer to be in the process of transforming you. Now the trainer says, "We're going to work out today between this Sunday and next Sunday. When we meet again for our training, this is what I want you to do, this is what I want you to eat, this is how much water I want you to drink, and what you do will facilitate what we are doing. You and I hook up formally once a week, but what you do all week long will facilitate what we started on Sunday when we met."

Let's say Monday through Saturday you disregard most of what the trainer went over with you on Sunday, but you never miss a Sunday training meeting. Every Sunday you go back to the trainer, and every Sunday the trainer is telling you the same thing, but you're not changing. You're not getting stronger; you're not getting more muscular. In fact, you gained weight and you want to know why since you go every single week to the trainer. The training is not changing you because the trainer understands that if meeting the trainee formally on Sunday is going to bring about the change, you have to follow his or her commandments. You have to fulfill the expectations. Not because they're trying to burden you; they're trying to change you. In order for Sunday to do what Sunday is designed to do, Monday through Saturday has to cooperate with it. He says, "My commandments are not burdensome when they are mixed with love."

The reason why you may seem overwhelmed with the 613 commandments is that you're following a rule book and not pursuing a relationship. Yes, there's going to be expectations, but the expectations are going to take away the fat, build up the muscle, and increase the health. When you find out that the expectations are going to do that, the expectations become a joy on a journey and not a burden for life. People who are burdened with God's expectations either are not pursuing a relationship and are just doing rules for rules' sake, or they are not serious about what God is asking for as the first and foremost. He says, "I want it all."

Unfortunately today, so many of us from pulpit to pew and back again are part-time Christians wanting a full-time salary. We're part-time saints. God can have a little of this; he can have a little of that. A little bit of my heart, little bit of my mind, little bit of my legs, little bit of my hands. I'm going to give you this, but now I need a full-time job even though you only got a part-time saint. The keyword here is *all*. He wants the full allocation of your life, which means saying no to the world that hasn't helped you out that much anyway. He wants it all. Not with ritual, not in abstract terms; it's concrete because you want this loving relationship with him and that's why you obey his commandments. Not just for commandment-keeping sake like the Pharisees, but because you want to pursue the greatest commandment of them all: You want to love me.

Here it is: What is the greatest commandment? The greatest commandment is to love the Lord God with all you got; and if you find out next week you got more than you know you had this week, then give him that too. You become consumed with the love of God, the relationship reflected by the commandment-keeping. Look at what happens; something happens here. Notice what he says in verse 38, "This is the great and foremost commandment" (Deuteronomy 6:4–5). Verse 39 says, "The second is like it." Now wait a minute. Whoa hold it. The lawyer didn't ask about number two. He asked, what is the greatest commandment?—singular. He never asked, what is the greatest first and second commandment? What are the top two? He didn't ask about that. He said, "I just want to know about one commandment. What is the greatest?" Jesus answers a question he didn't ask. He didn't ask about two; he asked about one; but then Jesus comes up and says, "Let me tell you about another that you didn't ask about." He says, "The second is like it."

The reason I have to talk to you about number two is if number one stops with number one, you haven't finished with number one because number two is inseparable from number one. If you do number one, you cannot ignore number two; because if you ignore number two, you don't understand number one. It's like hinges on a door. When you have two hinges on a door, for that door to swing right both hinges must be working. It's going to be crooked otherwise. Look, you get together with God, you're like a monk, you're a monastery, you're doing Christian yoga, and you're just spending time with God, you're meditating, you're reading your Bible, you're praying, and you're doing all that. That's wonderful, because you're trying to cultivate this private relationship with God. Then Jesus jumps in the middle of it and says, "Let me tell you about two." Because it is like the first one.

Jesus says, "And you are to love your neighbor as yourself." He now adds Leviticus 19:18 to Deuteronomy 6:4 and 5. Well, let me just read 1 John for you again. First John 4:12 says, "No one has seen God at any time. If we love one another, God abides in us and his love is perfected in us." First John 4:20 says, "If someone says I love God and hates his brother, he is a liar. For one, he does not love his brother, whom he has seen, cannot love God, whom he has not seen." This is the commandment we have from him: the one who loves God should love his brother also. Chapter 5 verse 1, "Whoever believes that Jesus is the Christ is born of God and whoever loves the Father loves the child born in him. By this we know that we love the children of God when we love God and observe his commandments."

As Romans 13:8–10 says, "Love does not do wrong to his neighbor." What it says is that this second piece is tied to the first piece. Your love for God will be spiteful if it does not involve others. He says the love of God abides, hangs out in us, as we are connected to others, because he wants somebody else to feel the love you have for you. Now, whether you know it or not, you love you. I know you got self-esteem issues. We live in a day where everybody got self-esteem issues, but even with your issues you love you.

Let me show you how much you love you. When you get hungry, you eat. You don't say to you to get over it, tough, deal with it, because you love you. When you get thirsty, you go get you something to drink because you love you. When you get tired, you will find you a bed because you love you some sleep for you. When you are sick, you go find you some medicine or find you a doctor, because you love some you feeling better. You know what? You love you. The Bible assumes you love you.

We got folks trying to go find themselves. The best way to find you is to stop looking for you, that's what the Bible says. The Bible says, until a seed falls to the ground and dies, it shall no wise discover itself. Stop hunting for something, because if you don't know who you are, how do you know when you will discover you, because you don't know what you're looking for. He says the way you do this: assume that you love you. You can just assume that by the things you do for you. He says, the way you go to experience the love I want you to have for me is in transferring what you do for you to the benefit of somebody outside of you.

Let's put it this way. A young lady from our church came to me a few months ago and asked, "Pastor, how can I draw nearer to God?" My answer was, "Help some other folks draw nearer to God." The way you can draw nearer to God is help somebody draw nearer to God, because God is going to boomerang that thing back to you. Your desire for a love for God is shared with another. God will abide in that spirit and bring it back to you—in asking you to connect with somebody else, to get with a group, to be a host. I'm not just asking you to facilitate a meeting or to do a program; I'm asking you to get on board with what God is trying to do for you, and that it'll give you a greater experience with him that he will not give you if you're a lone-ranger Christian or an isolated saint.

He says, "And the second is like it." He says, "These two," which really are two sides of one coin, "are so potent"(verse 40)."On these two commandments depend the whole law and the prophets." Now watch this: he says, "On these two." You only asked him about one, but I got to tell you about two in order for you to get the whole picture. He says, "On these two hangs the whole Old Testament"—including the 613 commandments, so let's go. He's got 613 statues and ordinances that derive from Ten Commandments, but the Ten Commandments derive from two commandments. You remember when Moses went up the mountain to get the Ten Commandments? He was handed two tablets. Not one, two. One tablet, an obligation to God. Second tablet, an obligation to others. Why? Because the two tablets make up the one story and he says everything hinges on these two.

Let's put it another way. Jesus says, if you get these two right, you will fulfill all 613. You say, I come to church every Sunday. I can't remember all these sermons. I can't remember last week's sermon. How do I keep up with all the Bible? There's sixty-six books; there are all these pages, all these principles, all these guidelines. I can't keep up with that. Jesus said, "If I can get you to remember these two—if I just get you to the hang out with these two, you will cover the whole Bible." I got good news for you. Even though it depresses me to know you forget my sermons week by week (I do have issues with that!), the good news I have for you today is if you just remember two, Jesus says everything else hangs on them. You are to love him with everything that you got, and you are to transfer that to others; and when you do, you got the whole Bible starting to live inside you, because he said the whole Scripture depends on just these two.

I want to close by telling you a little story where Jesus brings the two together in a most remarkable way in John 21. This helps me. This helps me pastor the Oak Cliff Bible Fellowship. That means I just got to get everybody in here to do two things. If everybody just does two things, this is going to be a congregation that's got the whole Bible, because everything feeds into these two things. Peter told the Lord in Luke 22, "I love you more than all the other disciples. I'm your main man here. Nobody is more committed to you than me." That's what he told Jesus. Jesus, when he heard him say that, said, "Shut up, shut up, shut up. Before tomorrow morning when the rooster crows, you will have denied me three times." Now if I was Peter, I would have found a Holiday Inn or something. I would have hid. Peter said, "I love you more than these." Jesus says, "Your pride is your downfall, and so before tomorrow morning, before the rooster crows, you will deny me three times."

You know the story. When they arrested Jesus, and they said that Peter was Jesus, he denied him once, then he denied him twice; then it says the third time he denied him with cursing—meaning that whenever you cuss, that means you want to make it emphatic. I told you, I don't blankety-blankety-blank know the man! When Peter denied Jesus the third time, it says, "And the rooster crowed." It says, "Peter ran outside and wept bitterly." That means he wailed. Have you ever done something in your life that you thought you would never do? You said, I'd never do that, and you wind up doing it. God's revealing to you that you ain't all that, I'm not all that, we're not all that, even when we think we're all that. And Peter wept.

So destroyed was he by his failure, he walked away from the ministry God called him to and he went back to fishing. Went back to his old occupation where Jesus found him. Now watch this. That's the situation in John 21: he's back fishing after having denied the Lord; but what's interesting is that Jesus comes to where they're fishing. Peter just walked away because he's disappointed God, he's disappointed Jesus, he's disappointed himself, he's disappointed the other disciples. He is a failure. If there are any failures in the room, this text is for you. Jesus comes to the seashore where they are fishing and says, "Have you caught anything?" They've caught nothing. The word gets out that it's Jesus on the shore. Peter jumps in the water and starts swimming, because Jesus has come to him. He's too ashamed to go to Jesus, but Jesus has tracked him down. Not only has Jesus tracked him down (verse 12), Jesus is cooking breakfast—fish and eggs. Jesus said to them, "Come have some breakfast."

There's a whole story in itself how Jesus got the fish, but that's another story. They come into breakfast. They're sitting around eating their fish and eggs cooked by Jesus, and Jesus decides to ask Peter a question. In verse 15, it says that when they had finished breakfast, Jesus said to Simon Peter, "Simon, son of John, do you love me more than these?" What a way to open up a breakfast conversation. First of all, he calls him by his old name; he doesn't call him Peter. He done walked away from Peter; he done backed up to Simon. Have you ever messed up your name? He doesn't call him by his God-given name; he calls him by his human name. "Simon, son of John, do you still love me more than all these other disciples? Because that's what you told me. Before I got arrested, you told me you loved me more than these. Tell me how you're feeling right now. Do you love me more than these?"

Look at Peter's answer. Peter says, "Yes, Lord, you know I love you." Now, you can't see it in the English, but in the Greek those are two different words for love. The first time Jesus asks "Do you love Me" he uses the word *agape*. That's the same word where God wants us to love him and love our neighbors. It's that seeking the well-being of another, self-sacrificial love. When Jesus asked, "Do you love me?" Peter said, "I *phileo* you." This is where we get our name for Philadelphia, "brotherly love." Peter says, "I *like* you, because you ain't getting me out on that limb again. I messed up the last time. I ain't going with that *agape* stuff. So, I *like* you. That's the best I can give you right now, Jesus. I can give you brotherly-common love. I like you. I cannot say that I love you."

What does Jesus say? He says, "Tend my lamb." Wait a minute. "Jesus, I just told you I don't *agape* love you; I *phileo* like you." "Okay, wonderful Peter, we're going to send you over to the children's ministry. Tend my lambs." "You mean you're going to use me?" "Yeah, I'm going to use you, and the reason I'm going to use you is now you know who you are. You're not operating with that lying Christian self, talking about I love you, I love you, I love you. You say I like you, I like you, I like you; and that's the truth, the whole truth, and nothing but the truth, and I can't use you until you're willing to admit the truth, even if the truth is not what I want it to be, but it's the truth of where you are." God wants to start you where you are, in spite of where you come from.

Jesus says to him a second time, "Simon, son of John, do you *agape* me? Do you love me?" Peter says to him, "Yes, Lord, you know I *phileo* you." He says, "Tend my sheep." We done gone from lamb to sheep. "Let's go from the couple's ministry to the singles' ministry. We're going to do something with you now." Wait a minute. "You're going to give me a ministry? You're going to use me even though I don't *agape* you like you want to?" "Yes, because I can only use you when you come clean with what's wrong with you. As long as you carry on that façade, I can't do anything with you. If I would have said, 'Do you *agape* me, and you came back with I *agape* you, and both of us know you ain't there yet, you ain't ready yet; but now that you've been humbled because you faced your own sin and you faced your own humanity and you have now been brought low, and humbled yourself beneath the mighty hand of God, now I can do something with you." Oh, but it gets gooder.

Look at verse 17. Jesus says to Peter the third time, "Simon, son of John, do you love me?" Peter was grieved when he asked him the third time if he loved him. Peter says, "Lord, you know all things. You know that I love you." Jesus says to him, "Tend my sheep." Watch this. The third time Jesus asks if Peter loves him, he uses the Greek word *phileo*, not *agape*. Peter was grieved when he heard him ask, "Do you *phileo* me?" Why is he grieved? Because that's the third time. Peter denied the Lord three times, so when Jesus asked him the third time, it reminded him of the three times when he had a few days before denied the Lord.

What is awesome about what grieved him was not that he remember what he did with the Lord, but that the Lord had to reduce his use of the word *love*. The first two times Jesus asked, "Do you *agape* me?" The third time Jesus asked, "Do you *phileo* me?" In other words: "Peter, you're not ready to come from where you are to where I am, but I'm willing to come from where I am to where you are. I will join you down there, and we will climb up here together because you have come clean with me, you have been honest with me, and therefore you and I can take out hands and—guess what? While you and I are grabbing the same word *phileo*, why don't you feed my sheep? I'm going to use you at the level that I can use until I can get you where I want you to be."

You know where all this happened? All this happened around a charcoal fire. It says, "Jesus was cooking on a charcoal fire." The word *charcoal* is only used twice in the New Testament: one time here in John 21, and when it says, "Peter, when he denied the Lord, warmed his hand over a charcoal fire." Jesus brings him back to the same spot where he fell down. He picks him up and the same fire where he messed up is the same fire where he got fixed up, because he was willing to come clean with Jesus Christ right where he was.

Even if you don't *agape* him today, I assume you don't hate him. That's why you're here. But you just may be at the place where you *like* him. Well, stop telling him that you love him because that's a lie. Tell him, "I like you, but I want to love you. Use me where I am and take me to where you want me to be, because you already know all things."

For additional sermon preparation help, see https://go.tonyevans.org/dr-tony-evans-free-christian-sermon-notes.

NOTES

1. For a complete explanation of the Free Market model, see Ted Haggard, *Dog Training, Fly Fishing, and Sharing Christ in the 21st Century: Empowering Your Church to Build Community through Shared Interests* (Nashville: Thomas Nelson, 2002).

2. Chris Shook and Kerry Shook, *One Month to Live: Thirty Days to a No-Regrets Life* (Colorado Springs: Waterbrook, 2012).

3. Chip Ingram, *Holy Ambition: Turning God-Shaped Dreams into Reality* (Chicago: Moody, 2010).

4. Rick Warren, *The Purpose-Driven Life: What on Earth Am I Here for?* (Grand Rapids: Zondervan, 2002).

5. Dave Ferguson and Warren Bird, *Hero Maker: Five Essential Practices for Leader to Multiply Leaders* (Grand Rapids: Zondervan, 2018), 41.

6. Carol S. Dweck, *Mindset: The New Psychology of Success* (New York: Random House, 2006), 6.

7. Ibid.

8. Ibid., 7.

9. Used with permission of David Gonzalez, Bay Hope Church, Lutz, Florida.

10. Used with permission of Elizabeth Scheib, Connect Church, Lawrence, Kansas.

11. This acronym comes from Steve Gladen's book, *Small Groups with Purpose*: H-have a heart for people; O-open your place (meet in a home, coffeehouse, restaurant, or workplace); S-serve a snack; T-turn on the DVD.

12. Used with permission of Elizabeth Scheib, Connect Church, Lawrence, Kansas.

13. Interview with Jack Welch and Bill Hybels, Global Leadership Summit, Willow Creek Community Church, South Barrington, IL, 2010.

14. Conversation on July 8, 2019, with Boyd Pelley, who was also a member of that coaching group.

15. Rick Rusaw and Brian Mavis, *The Neighboring Church* (Nashville: Thomas Nelson, 2016).

16. Ferguson and Bird, *Hero Maker*, 62.

17. Used with permission. Transcribed from the audio recording and edited for readability.

18. Used with permission of tonyevans.com. Transcribed from the audio recording and edited for readability.

About the Author

Allen White has devoted over thirty years to helping people find Christ, make meaningful connections, grow in their faith, and find fulfillment in ministry. He has successfully launched hundreds of groups at two churches as the associate pastor. He served at New Life Christian Center in Turlock, California for fifteen years, and at Brookwood Church in Simpsonville, South Carolina, for four years. Additionally, Allen has coached over fifteen hundred churches through onsite consultations, coaching groups, and courses.

A sought-after speaker, Allen has taught workshops for local churches and he has spoken at the Purpose Driven Church Conference at Saddleback Church, GroupLife Southwest, the BASS Church Workers Convention, the Leadership Centre-Canada, and many local churches.

Allen has a BA in Biblical Studies and Missions and an MDiv in Christian Education. Most of what he has learned has come through the "school of hard knocks." Many lessons have been learned through trying new things, failing, and trying again.

Allen lives with his wife, Tiffany, and their four children in Simpsonville, South Carolina. For more information about Allen's ministry, visit allenwhite.org.